YOU CAN'T TAKE IT WITH YOU

YOU CAN'T TAKE IT WITH YOU

FOOLPROOF TECHNIQUES *for* TIDYING UP LIKE THERE'S NO TOMORROW

MESSIE CONDO

BEST-SELLING AUTHOR OF
NOBODY WANTS YOUR SH*T

BLUESTONE
BOOKS

You Can't Take It with You.
Copyright © 2025 by Bluestone Books.
All rights reserved.

Any unauthorized duplication in whole or in part or dissemination of this edition by any means (including but not limited to photocopying, electronic devices, digital versions, and the internet) will be prosecuted to the fullest extent of the law.

Published by:
Bluestone Books
www.bluestonebooks.co

ISBN: 978-1-965636-07-7 (hardcover)
ISBN 978-1-965636-08-4 (ebook)

Printed in the United States of America
First Edition: 2025

10 9 8 7 6 5 4 3 2 1

TABLE *of* CONTENTS

6 *Introduction*

10 **CHAPTER 1**
Breathe.

19 **CHAPTER 2**
Find Your Motivation

33 **CHAPTER 3**
Get Your Head in the Game

43 **CHAPTER 4**
Learn How to Corral the Chaos

72 **CHAPTER 5**
Now, Tackle the Closet

94 **CHAPTER 6**
Upgrade Your Kitchen and Bath

111 **CHAPTER 7**
Find the Bottom of Your Inbox

129 **CHAPTER 8**
Sort Out the Sentimental Stuff

147 **CHAPTER 9**
Tie It Up in a Bow

168 **CHAPTER 10**
Keep Moving Forward

174 *Index*

THE TRUTH WILL SET YOU FREE

There comes a time in everyone's life when they think, "I have too much stuff." It's usually right after they trip over a box that won't fit in their closet. (Swearing may or may not be involved.) And it's often followed by watching dozens of decluttering videos, pulling everything they own out of said closet, and spending hundreds of dollars on organizational supplies. Spoiler alert: Hiding stuff in bins doesn't actually solve the problem of having too much stuff. Hence the tripping.

If you're currently nursing a bruised toe or two, or maybe even some existential dread, you've come to the right book. We're going to do this thing together using the decluttering method to end all decluttering methods: death cleaning. Yes, the name is mildly horrifying, especially for Americans, who will do anything to avoid dealing with death. We basically invented the midlife crisis and still think cryonics is a viable option. (It's not.) But this method is going to make your life better—hopefully, for many, many years to come.

What started as unspoken Swedish ethos has been helpfully distilled into a foolproof technique that cuts through all the guilt, panic, excuses, FOMO, and general stubbornness that keep you surrounded by stuff. The gist is this: Any decluttering you don't get around to before your time's up becomes someone else's problem. If the thought of your inevitable demise makes you squeamish, breathe through it. On the other side of that realization is freedom—the freedom to create a home and a life that truly reflect who you are.

We're going to do this thing together using the decluttering method to end all decluttering methods.

Death cleaning works for more than just end-of-life decluttering. Do you have a big move coming up? Are you ready to simplify your routines? Are you feeling overwhelmed? Do you fantasize about quitting your job and running away to a tiny cabin in the woods? Then this method is for you, too.

Now for the secret sauce, the key to clearing space, whittling down your possessions like a pro, making quick decisions, and saving everyone's sanity (including your own). You ready? Here it is, the truth: Nobody wants your stuff. Not even you. Did you just glance around the room indignantly? I get it. You've got a lot of great stuff. But you're also holding on to a lot of other stuff just because you think you should. And when you're gone, your friends and family will hold on to it because they think they should. See the problem?

It's time to break the cycle of stuff.

It's time to break the cycle of stuff. Don't you want to live your life surrounded by a thoughtfully selected collection of things you love instead of heirlooms you don't use, cables you can't identify, and moth-eaten baby clothes your kids don't want? Who wouldn't? And don't you want to free your friends and family from the burden of dealing with your stuff after you're gone? Of course you do. You're not a monster. So let's do this thing!

⸙HAVE WE MET BEFORE?⸙

If you bought and enjoyed *Tidy the F*ck Up* and *Nobody Wants Your Sh*t*, thank you! Hopefully you're back because you can't get enough of my delightfully acerbic wit and not because your stuff has taken over your house again like a pack of wet gremlins. Even if that's the case, fear not—I've got plenty more tips to help you get your life (and death) together once and for all. I've even tidied up my language to make sure the message comes through loud and clear. We're in this thing together!

BREATHE.

YOU'RE PROBABLY LOOKING AROUND YOUR HOUSE RIGHT NOW, taking in the full breadth of the stuff you've amassed over decades of life, and thinking, "Dear God, what have I done?" (You wouldn't have picked up this book—or, more likely, received it from a worried relative—if you were already a master of minimalism.) The realization that your days are numbered can be a pretty effective impetus, but it can also incite panic. Take a deep breath and avoid the urge to start pulling apart your closet. We're going to take this one step at a time. Why? Because anxious decluttering isn't productive or sustainable. The adrenaline only lasts so long, and then you find yourself exhausted, unmotivated, and sleeping on the couch because your bed is covered with every piece of clothing you own. (Ask me how I know.) No, you're not ready yet. But keep reading, and you'll get there.

CLUTTER RUNS DEEP

You've tried to declutter before and it didn't stick. So, what makes this time different? The fact that we're not just going to throw things in bins and hope for the best. We're going to tackle the deeper reasons your past attempts have been less than successful. Clutter is like an iceberg—what you see on the surface is just the tip. And if you're not careful, what lies beneath can sink you.

> *Clutter is like an iceberg—what you see on the surface is just the tip. And if you're not careful, what lies beneath can sink you.*

Everything in your home is the result of a heady mixture of social conditioning, marketing, upbringing, expectation, sentimentality, desire, and personal quirks. If your parents were known to throw out the old "waste not, want not," you're more likely to hold on to stuff long past its prime. (One more thing to blame on Mom.) If you spend your free time scrolling through socials, you'll be bombarded by ads tailor-made to trigger your "buy now" reflex. If your grandmother loved that ugly velvet clown painting and you loved her, you might soldier through your coulrophobia and hang it up. (Probably in the attic, though. Facing the wall.) In other words, it's not your fault! It is your problem, though. Sorry.

But knowing *why* you're loathe to let go can help you do it once and for all. So, as you take in your lifetime's worth of stuff, take the time to breathe through your feelings and figure out what's causing them. It's far more effective than instantly succumbing to those feelings and shoving your collection of nice boxes back in the closet.

THE FIVE STAGES OF DEATH CLEANING

Not everything you own requires a therapy session. Those tees your money-grubbing company gave you instead of Christmas bonuses? Buh-bye. (Why do you still have those?) That funky-smelling eyeshadow you bought for a party five years ago? Trash. But you may be surprised to find you're more attached to that box of unreadable floppy disks than you realize. If you're having trouble pitching things, you may need to grieve them. No, really. Emotional problems require emotional solutions.

Just like the five stages of grief, the emotional phases of decluttering aren't necessarily linear. You might be deep into acceptance when you come across those old model airplanes your dad left you, and suddenly you're bargaining again. That's OK. The goal here isn't to become a decluttering machine. It's to chip away at the clutter until you find your personal sweet spot, and then make a plan for what happens to it next.

DENIAL

You built this cluttered home LEGO brick by LEGO brick. Why should you have to change it? It's not that bad. You've seen way worse. That's the denial talking. When the initial decluttering panic/thrill wears off, you're going to start dragging your heels on this whole thing. It's normal. But when you start to feel resistance around donating those work clothes you haven't worn in ten years or ditching those greeting cards from people you don't even talk to anymore, breathe through it.

Remember, death cleaning isn't about paring down to a joylessly sparse space. It's about choosing how you want to spend the rest of your life. If keeping that sexy sheath dress from your boardroom days makes you happy, go for it. Better yet, make a lunch date with a friend and actually wear the dress. But if you're more of a beach bum now, embrace that. You'll feel lighter, and some future boss-lady will love the wardrobe upgrade.

ANGER

Why did your kids leave all of their stuff at your house when they moved out? Who has time for this? Why do you care what happens to your stuff when you're gone? That's not your problem. Welcome to anger. Sometimes it's irrational, but sometimes it's perfectly reasonable. It's just not very helpful (unless you end up rage-cleaning the basement). When it hits, come back to those deep breaths. Do not,

⸱GUILT⸱

Whether you're clinging to Great Aunt Tilley's Christmas dishes or a pile of cellphones with buttons (*gasp*), guilt may be the common denominator. It's one of the main reasons we hold on to stuff we don't want or use. It's also a big reason we pawn that stuff off on other people who don't want it. Then it becomes their problem. (How very adult of us.) If you can give yourself a break, you can get past the guilt and do what's best for everyone—even if that's letting some lucky thrifter enjoy Tilley's dishes.

for example, toss that box you tripped over into the trash without looking at what's inside it unless you want to spend the next six months saying, "Why can't I find my passport?"

BARGAINING

What if you get rid of that printer cable and they stop making Wi-Fi printers? You swear you'll get rid of two things for every new item you buy from now on. Maybe you should just hold on to those baby clothes—Marcy might change her mind. Ah, bargaining. In the case of decluttering, it often shows up in the form of rationalization. When you start making excuses for why you should keep something when it makes no actual sense to keep it, you know you're in the bargaining stage. (The word *should* is a big hint.) Only logic can get you out. You're never going to need that printer cable, that's just an excuse to buy more stuff, and you should definitely respect someone who says, "I don't want that." That last part is death cleaning 101, so we'll be circling back to it later.

DESPAIR

What's the point? You could live another fifty years and you wouldn't have time to get through all this stuff. Let them

BREATHE.

haul it all to the dump when you die. At some point during this process, you're going to want to quit. Let's be real—at many points. You've spent decades accruing all this stuff. It's going to take some doing to get through it all. When the urge to throw in the towel hits, take a break! There's a reason we're doing this a little bit at a time. The point of this is to make your life (and, yes, your *eventual* death) better. Don't let the clutter drive you crazy.

ACCEPTANCE
It's not going to get easier the longer I put it off. This room will feel so spacious without all this stuff in it. I'm so over

> ### ⋛ DECISION PARALYSIS ⋛
> Bargaining often goes hand in hand with decision paralysis, which is an elaborate term for overthinking. *What if you get rid of something and regret it? What if you need it? What if it's worth something?* The trick is tuning out the what-ifs and trusting your best judgment. (Don't worry—the more you do it, the easier it gets.) And if you're really not sure, ask yourself whether you can easily and cheaply replace the thing should you suddenly need it. Sure, it's annoying to spend money on something you used to own. But holding on to a box of printer cables for forty years when you could be using that space for things you actually do want is way worse.

worrying about this. Acceptance is the bread and butter of death cleaning. It's coming to terms with the fact that you're not going to live forever and letting it inspire you to take control of your life instead of letting it send you into a crippling spiral of existential dread. Once you accept that, one way or another, your stuff will end up in someone else's hands (and sometimes the trash), everything gets easier.

Once you accept that, one way or another, your stuff will end up in someone else's hands (and sometimes the trash), everything gets easier.

ON THE OTHER SIDE

Getting your life together even just a tiny bit has a huge upside for your mental and physical well-being. There are the obvious benefits, like more space, more money, fewer bruises, and an easier time finding the scissors when you need them. Then there's the fact that you'll have more time, make quicker decisions, and feel a sense of accomplishment that can't be beat. But what will strike you the most is the peace of mind. Studies show that

BREATHE.

decluttering can actually help you feel less anxious, sleep better, and have more energy. So put down that espresso and pick up those ratty, grass-stained socks (which, to be clear, go in the trash).

TAKE ACTION

The point of this book is to get you moving and motivated, so we're going to end every chapter with a few things you can do right now.

- **SERIOUSLY, BREATHE.** Before you do any decluttering—now, later, whenever—take three slow, deep breaths. Taking five seconds to start from a place of calm (versus sheer panic) makes a huge difference.

- **DETERMINE YOUR BASELINE.** Look around your place and sit with whatever you're feeling for a few minutes. Are you annoyed? Angry? Excited? Identifying your emotions now will help you recognize and deal with them while you declutter.

- **CHOOSE SOMETHING TO LOOK FORWARD TO.** Decide which benefit of decluttering speaks to you most, and remember it whenever this stuff starts to get on your nerves.

FIND YOUR MOTIVATION

EVERY FEW STEPS ALONG THIS JOURNEY, you're going to ask yourself why on Earth you're doing this, like an actor melodramatically bellowing, "What's my *motivation*?" But you'll be prepared for those moments of doubt, because you're going to get clear on your motivation right now. It's not going to be some trite decluttering mantra, either. Your motivation has to be your own signature cocktail of reasons if it's going to work for you. Whether you respond better to positive reinforcement or need someone to knock some sense into you, there's something here for everyone. Collect the ones that resonate with you and keep them handy. And watch out for falling excuses—like a rock to the noggin, they'll stop you in your tracks. It's a lot harder to concentrate on decluttering when you've been concussed by your own ego.

ME-FOCUSED MOTIVATORS

The benefits of death cleaning aren't all altruistic. This is as much for you as it is for those who stand to inherit your stuff. The me-focused motivators are about reclaiming your space. We spend the majority of our lives collecting more and more stuff. We spend a lot less of them thinking about whether that stuff still serves us. Now's your chance.

Decluttering is self-care.
Prioritize your happiness.

YOU WANT TO LOVE YOUR SPACE

Decluttering is one of those things that never quite makes it to the top of the to-do list. You have to clean the refrigerator or it will stink. You have to do laundry unless you want to wear your bathing suit as underwear to work on Monday. You have to mow the lawn before HOA Karen comes knocking. But there's no tangible downside to delaying your decluttering efforts a little while longer, right? Wrong. The downside is you don't get to fully enjoy your home. You're too busy tripping over boxes, searching for things you need in a growing number of junk drawers, or eating on your lap because your kitchen table is covered in junk mail, receipts, and groceries you've yet to put away.

Decluttering is self-care. Prioritize your happiness. How? By deciding what you want your home to look and feel like and then removing everything that's standing in the way of having that. If you want to savor delicious homemade meals at a candlelit table, then you need to whip your kitchen and dining room into shape. If you want a little meditation space in your bedroom, you're going to have to rehome the laundry chair. (You know— that chair you never sit in because it's covered in clothes that you haven't put away because your drawers are too full. Yep, that means dealing with the overflowing drawers, too. Noticing a pattern?) Those are the trade-offs. But they're worth it if it means getting what you really want. So? What do you want?

YOU'VE CHANGED

Clinging to that yarn you bought when you were into knitting for a hot minute or the shot glass you got on your guys' trip to Vegas out of stubbornness and principle isn't

⸓YOUR TECH HAS CHANGED, TOO⸓

You know what else evolves? Tech. If you're still coveting your huge collection of DVDs but haven't dusted off your DVD player in years, it might be time to accept that you prefer the convenience of streaming. Your local library would probably be thrilled to get an influx of mid-'90s rom-coms—all you have to do is ask. And bonus, you'll still have access to Meg Ryan's greatest hits through that same library should you get the urge. Some even have DVD players you can rent. *Hint, hint.*

doing you any favors. Try as you might, you can't relive your glory days via glassware. And it's a little sad when you look wistfully at that cheap souvenir. You're not that person anymore. Human beings change, grow, and evolve. (Ideally, anyway. If that process doesn't sound familiar, you may need a different kind of self-help book.)

The stuff you surround yourself with should fuel the life you live now. Maybe Old You used to host magazine-worthy dinner parties with napkin rings and place cards, and Current You eats Chinese food out of takeout containers after a heated game of pickleball with those same friends. Both versions of You are great, but only one of You needs table settings for twelve. Declutter for the

You you are now. You deserve it. Cherish the memories, toss the plastic (into a properly coded recycle bin).

YOU'RE NOT GETTING ANY YOUNGER

Now, I don't know you. You could be a sixty-year-old weightlifter with the energy of a fifteen-year-old cheerleader. But me? I'm tired. I'd rather sit on the couch with a binge-worthy show and a tasty snack than lug boxes back and forth from storage. And I only have myself to blame if all my belongings can't fit within the confines of my living space. Note: I didn't say *my attic space* or *my basement*. The camouflaged bear trap that is what we lovingly refer to as "storage space" is a topic for later, after you've warmed up your decluttering muscles. For now, know this: Decluttering doesn't get easier the longer you put it off. And if you keep buying stuff (as we all do), it actually gets harder. So start now and save Future You a backache.

THEM-FOCUSED MOTIVATORS

If you're a natural-born people pleaser and susceptible to guilt, these them-focused motivators can help you keep your eye on the prize: continuing to people-please in the afterlife. (There has to be some kind of bonus for that, right? Like spectral extra credit?) Kidding. Guilt is just empathy that someone has touched with their sticky jam hands. That guilt-jam belongs to someone else. It's social conditioning, or it's other people's hang-ups and expectations. Remembering that can help you get unstuck. We're not using guilt or anxiety to motivate you to declutter here. We're just tapping into your natural drive to do right by the people you care about.

IT'S A LOT

The fact that this whole decluttering thing feels like *a lot* might be exactly what's deterring you from doing it, but it should also be your biggest motivator. Imagine if someone else had to declutter your stuff—stuff they have no warm, fuzzy feelings about—on top of work, childcare, and life. *That's* a lot. Not leaving your mess for others to clean up is the bare minimum. You made it. You clean it up. And don't even think about saying you don't have time. *They* don't have time.

The good news is that no one is expecting you to square away a lifetime's worth of stuff in one night. You can inch your way toward a streamlined space one fifteen-minute decluttering session at a time. You just have to make it a priority. Maybe you spend fifteen fewer minutes doomscrolling. (Bonus: That's like decluttering your brain.)

Not leaving your mess for others to clean up is the bare minimum.

DECLUTTERING IS A GIFT

Do you want to be the benevolent hero in your loved ones' stories, or the villain who left them a house, garage, and storage shed full of stuff to deal with? Do you want them shedding tears of exhaustion and frustration as well as sadness? (If you do, them-focused motivators are not for you. Therapy might be, though.) Making sure your kids don't have to declutter your home while they grieve your loss (or help you downsize into a swanky retirement villa) is the greatest gift you can give them. Way better than that box of their kindergarten art projects you've been saving for them. The items that remain after you've pared down and lovingly recycled those fingerpaint portraits will hold real meaning for them, because they were actually important to you.

MESS-FOCUSED MOTIVATORS

You're sick of bruised shins and tumbling storage containers and trying to find literally anything in your overstuffed closets. You can feel the irritation bubbling up as you inch closer and closer to your clutter limit. That's when you turn to these mess-focused motivators and let them push you over the edge. On the other side are clear kitchen counters, a capsule wardrobe you love, and the ability to breathe again. (OK, the capsule wardrobe might be a little ambitious. But your closets will definitely be better than they were.)

YOU'VE GONE CLUTTER BLIND

One of the biggest gripes I hear about death cleaning is the idea that people have to cater to the needs of others in their own home. I get it. You've filled your home with things you loved—at the time. But after a while, all of your carefully selected decor starts to blend in with its surroundings. You no longer notice those seashells you brought home from the Outer Banks or the action figures you outbid DCAddict69 for (until they're covered by a thick coating of dust, that is). Maybe they don't have the same appeal as they used to. Maybe you've moved on to other interests. Or maybe you need to make an effort to enjoy them more. Death cleaning just helps you ask the questions. What you do with the answers is up to you.

Notice what you're not noticing anymore.

Keep in mind, your beloved decor isn't the only stuff taking up residence in your home. You also walk right past those piles of unopened mail, papers you keep meaning to file, and odds and ends that don't seem to have a place of their own. When that happens, you know it's time to take back control of your house and make those action figures work for the space they take up. Notice what you're not noticing anymore. Everything in your house should add to your comfort or joy. The trick is realizing when that's not the case and making a change instead of stubbornly digging in your heels just because. But, surely, you wouldn't know anything about that.

THE MENTAL LOAD OF MESSINESS IS HEAVY

If you've scrolled on social media or have argued over dishwasher duties in couples therapy within the last few years, you've probably heard the term *mental load*. It's the cognitive, emotional, and energetic work it takes to manage a household—among all the other things. And every item in your home adds to it. You have to organize it, clean it, maintain it, and remember it exists so you can use it. (If you're thinking "no sweat," go look at the expiration dates of your pantry items.) The more stuff you have to manage, the less bandwidth you have to focus on what really matters. Like spending quality time with loved ones, or beating your brother at Wordle.

All of those things you're keeping "just in case" may seem comforting to you in this moment, but they won't

⋛SCARCITY MINDSET⋚

All joking aside, scarcity mindset can cause some real problems when it comes to decluttering. People whose families passed down Depression-era thinking or those who have experienced tricky financial situations firsthand are more likely to struggle with this hyperfocus on lack. They might keep an iron grip on their things because they're genuinely worried they won't have something when they need it or the money to replace it. If that's you, don't hesitate to reach out for help, whether it's from a therapist, a friend, or a sibling who can remind you how resilient you are (while lovingly prying that burned-out vacuum cleaner out of your hand).

be comforting to the people who have to clean up after you. The extra place settings, the not-quite-dead-yet batteries, the untouched dumbbells, the bits of gift wrap you've saved—they're just junk to your loved ones. (I get it, though. It's hard to let go of a really nice ribbon.) The truth is, that "comfort" is costing you. It's adding to your mental load, it's taking up your precious space, and it's keeping you from moving forward with your life. Are the dumbbells worth it?

YOU'RE SICK OF CLEANING

The seasonal clothing has to be washed (unless you like smelling like a plastic bin), the picture frames have to be dusted, the flameless candles all need new batteries . . . the list goes on and on. Aren't you sick of it? How many years of your life would you get back if you didn't have to clean, care for, sort, and put away all the things you own? (If you're feeling scientific, you can time your next whole-house dusting session and do the math.) Some cleaning is inevitable. But it's a lot easier to tidy a shelf that doesn't hold a bunch of dusty picture frames. Why not upload those photos to the cloud and switch to a digital frame that will rotate through them? Then you have one thing to dust instead of twenty, your photos are safely backed up, and those physical copies can get neatly tucked away—or tossed in the recycle bin if you're really feeling ambitious. And that's just one example. Think of what else you could consolidate or downsize to make your life easier. Once you've decluttered, you can spend less time cleaning and more time doing yoga with baby goats, or whatever it is you like to do.

YOU'LL PROBABLY MOVE

Odds are good that you're going to move at least once more in your lifetime (even if you've defiantly cried, "They're going to carry me out of this house feet first!"). Life happens. You get a new job, your kid moves away and you follow, you decide to downsize, or you heed the siren call of a sunny retirement in the South of France. And when you do, decluttering suddenly rockets to the top of your to-do list. But dealing with a lifetime of clutter on a tight deadline is no joke. If you leave it until you absolutely *have* to do it, you'll end up panic-packing and throwing stuff you're not even sure you like into boxes. Then what happens? You have to deal with it in your new home. Worse, you might frantically toss cherished items in the trash and regret it later. (Man, I miss those mix-tapes.)

Start before you have to, work a little at a time, and moving becomes a breeze. Or as much of a breeze as uprooting your entire life can be. Alternatively, if you're someone who needs a sense of urgency to get stuff done, set an imaginary move-out date and treat it like it's carved in stone. You can even go the extra mile and imagine the space you're "moving" to, which will help you get clear on what you want and make quicker decisions. It's the ultimate hack for procrastinators. (More on that later— I got you, my fellow procrastinators.)

No matter how much time you have, it's running out. Start carving out more space for joy today.

YOU COULD GET HIT BY A BUS

This motivator gets special billing because it's basically the crux of death cleaning. Is it morbid to think you might be cleaved from this mortal plane at any moment? Yes. Is it effective? Also yes. No one knows how much time they have left. Hopefully it's a lot. And surely, you want every minute of it to be filled with joy, peace, and love. So, you might be asking yourself, why would you spend *any* of it decluttering? Because, crazy as it seems, decluttering is not the opposite of joy. Decluttering is joyful. It's clearing the way for what you really want. It's taking back your time and space. It's sharing your passions with others while you're alive. And it's letting your loved ones grieve you when you're gone *without* having a pile of old magazines fall over on them. No matter how much time you have, it's running out. Start carving out more space for joy today.

TAKE ACTION

Are you starting to feel that desire to declutter percolate? Good. Here are some ways to turn up the heat.

- **MAKE YOUR MOTIVATION STICK.** Which reasons for decluttering are speaking to you? Write them on sticky notes and leave them where you can see them— maybe with a big arrow pointing toward that stack of papers you've been meaning to go through.

- **FIGURE OUT WHAT YOU WANT.** What does your ideal space look like? What's getting in the way of you having that? Make a list, then start chipping away at what's not working for you.

- **START DECLUTTERING!** We're going to keep easing into this stuff, but that shouldn't stop you from cleaning out that junk drawer that's been calling your name. When inspiration strikes, make the most of it.

GET YOUR HEAD IN THE GAME

YOU'VE SPENT SOME TIME tidying up your subconscious. You've started training your brain to see clutter for what it is. You've seen some of your go-to excuses dissolve into goo. Hopefully, all this introspection has got you feeling fired up and ready to reclaim your space. Just hold on to that energy for this next part: wrapping your head around the actual decluttering. A lesser mortal might be tempted to let the sheer enormity of the task crush their soul and go back to binge-watching *White Lotus*. But not you. You're better than that. (Probably.) You got yourself into this mess, and you're going to get yourself out of it. Don't worry—we're still going to take this one step at a time. And when you're feeling overwhelmed, remember this: you did not buy this book just to add it to your pile of unfinished projects. Dig in.

GET REAL

This is your one wild and precious life. I want you to fill it with whatever stuff makes you happy. Selfishly cling to the things that bring you joy. But be honest—not everything in your home fits that lofty description. In fact, most things don't. Some of those things are perfunctory— think: toilet brushes or screwdrivers. (Though, as someone who's put a lot of modular furniture together, a power screwdriver will change your life.) The others might include impulse buys you regret, gifts you feel too guilty to unload, and things you've outgrown (physically, mentally, *and* emotionally). Once you chip away at those extraneous things, you finally get to enjoy your space on your terms. The fact that your loved ones don't have to wade through a garage full of broken beach chairs, long-forgotten holiday decorations, and expired chemical solvents is just a really big bonus.

TAKE STOCK

If you counted every single thing in your home—every piece of clothing, every book, every sauce packet, and every tiny shampoo bottle you brought home from hotels—it would total in the tens of thousands. And whether you realize it or not, all that stuff is taking up space in your brain as well as in your home. Yes, even the sauce packets. So the goal isn't just to discover what's been lurking in the recesses of your closets and drawers. It's to become fully aware of all the things occupying your life.

All that stuff is taking up space in your brain as well as in your home.

First things first: take inventory. This goes beyond rifling through storage spaces and discovering those old roller skates you've been holding on to since eighth grade. Even artwork and decor you bought and loved recently becomes background noise as your brain gets used to its presence. You need to take stock of it all. How do you do that? Well, you could whip out that pretty notebook you've never written in or pull up a spreadsheet on your

> **⸙HOLD UP!⸙**
>
> You've probably already started scanning the room around you. I love the enthusiasm. But this inventory isn't just a thoughtful exercise in perspective. It's your first pass. Read through the next section to learn how you can make the most of it. (Unless you've already spotted some things you know you want to toss. Then go do that and come back. I'm not here to clutter-block you.)

computer and start tallying up everything you own. It would certainly be eye-opening. But that smacks of work.

I don't know about you, but I'm a "work smarter, not harder" kind of organizer. Luckily, there's an easier way: take a visual inventory, one nook or cranny at a time. (Disclaimer: It's not entirely visual. You will have to use your hands. Don't be nitpicky.) Open a drawer and really look at each object inside. Peek in a closet and pay special attention to the things you have to push past to do a full scan. Look over the surface of your dresser and notice every loose penny, pair of tweezers, and crumpled receipt. You'll get a real idea of what you have and, more than likely, you'll start to feel exhausted by the weight of it all.

Don't let it overwhelm you. Don't let the stuff win. Let it motivate you. As I said in *Tidy the F*ck Up*, you're not going to get down to the business of decluttering if you look around your home and think, "This is fine." You have to be so sick of your own . . . poppycock . . . that you can't stand it anymore. (Obviously, I did not say "poppycock.") And seeing just how much stuff you actually have is a forceful shove in that direction.

GO WITH YOUR GUT

When you go through your things, you'll automatically start differentiating between the ones you can't live without and the ones you couldn't care less about. You can't help it. So take advantage of it! This is the perfect time to do some quick-and-dirty decluttering.

The key to making quick decisions is tuning into your gut reactions. If you're someone who can't even decide between toothpaste flavors without hitting up online reviews, you're not alone. We live in an age of instant gratification *and* validation. Why trust your gut when you can text ten friends for their opinions or live vicariously through other people's threads? But the more you lean on your own intuition, the easier it gets. That's the point of this first pass.

The goal is simple: As you notice each item, also notice your reaction to it. Are you smiling? Anxious? Disgusted? Dead inside? You're going to use those clues to make some rapid-fire decisions. This is not the time to hem and haw or stroll down memory lane. If you're not sure about something, move on. This initial phase is about getting the easy stuff out of the way and building some momentum. Think: old printer cables, those pants that never fit, the shaving cream your ex left at your place. (Actually, there's no reason not to use that shaving cream up. Free is free.) Having trouble staying on task? Set a timer. And keep the following questions in mind.

The more you lean on your own intuition, the easier it gets.

WHAT MADE YOU SMILE?

The things that bring a smile to your face *may* be keepers, but they still need to earn it. In the meantime, give those joy-inducing items a place to shine. Move that long-forgotten picture album to the coffee table, where you can thumb through it (instead of through your phone) while watching TV. Hang the sexy dress on your door so you

> ### ⸎ DO A BASE TIDY ⸎
>
> While you're doing this initial scan, you may as well recycle those crumpled receipts and put the tweezers away. You don't have to clean up like your boss is coming over for dinner. But moving any stragglers to the rooms where they actually belong, tossing any obvious trash, and doing some surface-level tidying up during this phase gives you a cleaner slate for the deeper decluttering. Plus, doing it as you scan the space makes it feel like less of a Chore with a capital C.

remember to wear it. Give that chipped mug you love a new life as a flowerpot. These things earn their keep by adding to your happiness, which they can't do from the back of a closet. But I have an ulterior motive here: Over time, you may notice you have no use for the dress, or that the mug doesn't hold the same appeal for you as it once did. Then you can send them on their way knowing that you gave it a shot.

WHAT'S BUGGING YOU?

Did you stop short when you opened that junk drawer? Did the chaos of your closet make you groan? This is a great time to figure out which areas of your home aren't working for you, and which are just plain annoying the crap out of you. If looking around your kitchen reminds you that untangling a whisk from twenty other kitchen tools makes you want to scream, that crock might be the first thing you tackle on your next pass. Starting with the areas that really get under your skin helps you stack some meaningful wins early on and build momentum—which you're going to need when you start sorting your clothes. (Get ready to blurt out, "Why does one person need this many socks?" a lot.)

WHAT MAKES YOU GO "MEH"?

At some point during this first pass, you're going to think, "Why do I even have this?" In the "out" pile it goes. Boom. Easy win. You're also going to find some items that you don't hate, you don't love, you don't use, but you're not sure you want to get rid of: That fancy garlic press you eschew in favor of an all-purpose microplane. The lotions you buy every winter but don't care enough to use. The sweater you loved in the store that you've since worn once. You had the best of intentions when you bought the thing. (Or some sweet gifter had the best of intentions when they bought it for you.) But it does nothing for you now. So why in the name of common sense are you hanging on to it? Because you spent money on it? Because you might need it someday? Because you're holding on to some idealized and unrealistic concept of who you are as a person? (Yeah, that one hits hard.) Stop torturing yourself. Instead, donate the garlic press to a thrift store and make some ambitious amateur chef's day—it's a win-win. And win-wins are the name of this decluttering game.

WHAT NEEDS YOUR ATTENTION?

Did you wince when you found the hole in your favorite tee that made you tuck it away in the first place? Did you groan when you pulled out the laptop that won't even turn on anymore? Those are good indications that you're not willing to spend the time, money, or effort to bring those things back to life. That's the bar. If something's broken, ripped, stained, or otherwise unusable and you can't be bothered to do something about it, out it goes. And don't even think about pulling the ol' "but I might..." You haven't yet, so you won't. And that's OK! You got a lot of enjoyment out of that tee. Nothing lasts forever.

The same goes for items both untouched and undusted. If you cringe at the tags still hanging from that pricey suit, or at the layer of film on your old record player, those items probably aren't integral to your life. If you're not sure, think of something that you can't live without—those cozy sweats you wear every weekend, that impressionist rendering of your dog, your emotional-support Mason jars (millennials get it). Use the things you love as a yardstick. If you don't love the record player as much as you love that painting, you probably won't miss it. But remember: This is an exercise in snap judgments. Don't drive yourself crazy. Just keep it moving through this first pass.

TAKE ACTION

Starting to hyperventilate? Breathe. It's not that serious. If nothing else, take these few small steps toward sanity.

- **SET UP SOME BOXES.** You should have at least three boxes (keep, donate, toss) to help you quickly sort your stuff. Under no circumstances will your stuff stay in these boxes. The point is to have *fewer* containers attacking your toes.

- **START YOUR INVENTORY.** Just start. Pick a room, then pick a small area of that room, and notice everything in it. That's it! You don't have to do the whole house today. Go at your own pace.

- **TACKLE ONE TINY SPOT.** Declutter the utensil crock or whatever other little accumulation of junk is bugging you, and don't stop until it looks and feels the way you really want it to.

LEARN HOW TO CORRAL THE CHAOS

CAN YOU JUST START TEARING THROUGH YOUR HOUSE in a caffeine-fueled frenzy and declutter the whole thing in one hectic weekend? Sure. But why would you want to? First of all, it sounds stressful. Second, you'll probably end up in traction on Monday, regretting your life choices. And to top it off, fugue-style decluttering is not nearly as effective as slow-and-steady decluttering. Planning things out *before* you drag everything out of your closet can be the difference between success and sitting in the fetal position next to a massive pile of shoes. So, we're going to work on deciding what you want your space to look like and how you're going to get it there. And because your decluttering style is as unique as your taste in '90s power ballads, I'm going to give you plenty of different approaches to try. Find what works for you and run with it.

What feels good to you?

REIMAGINE YOUR HOME

Some people are super intentional about their space, painstakingly picking out the perfect things to complement their plan for it and editing out what no longer works. But if you're reading this book, odds are good that you've been winging it. That's not to say you don't have a lovely, well-designed home—just that you probably never had $20,000 to throw down on an all-at-once, full-room makeover. Like most people, you added to your space one or two items at a time, sometimes shoving older items in a closet, and very occasionally sending some to thrift. Your space is an amalgam of every phase of your life. If that's the way you want it, great! No need to make changes. But it never hurts to imagine what your home could be.

VISUALIZE YOUR DREAM HOME

Take a few minutes right now to close your eyes and just daydream. Picture each room of your home in detail, one at a time. How do you want your space to look? More importantly, how do you want it to *feel*? Do you want your bedroom to be bright and loaded with hanging plants that fill you with joy? Do you want it to be Zen, monotone, minimalist, and calming? What feels good to you? Try to filter out any ideas of what you think you should want, or what you think the idealized version of you would want. If you've never before in your life so much as stretched your neck, a dedicated yoga space is probably not for you. (But who knows? Maybe try a class first.)

PUT IT IN WRITING

Once you've got some ideas about what you want your space to be, write them down. (We all know better than to trust our memories at this point, right?) Whether you make a list, an architectural floor plan, or an artistic rendering, get your thoughts down on paper. Then compare your vision for each space with the actual space. What's different? What needs to change in order for your home to feel the way you want it to feel? And no, "I need to win the lottery" is not an acceptable answer.

⚡VISUALIZATION AIDS⚡

If you're one of the roughly 4 percent of people who lives with aphantasia (the inability to see images in your mind) or you just need a little inspo, you can use photos and illustrations to help you hone your style. Go old-school and make a mood board out of magazine clippings, or do it online using social-media folders, design software, or digital vision-board sites. The goal is the same: get super clear on what you want from your space.

This is about being intentional with your space, not making a wish list for your next trip to the outlets. (But go ahead and make that list. We both know you're not going to stop shopping. Keeping a running list of your wants will at least help you stay focused when you're in the store. Plus, there's a chance the urge will pass before you get there.) Which items in your space are not contributing to your vision for it? Which are detracting from it? By editing those things out (read: donating them), you create your happy place *and* save your descendants from inheriting the kitschy cow-themed accessories currently keeping you from your soothing Scandinavian-style kitchen.

MAKE SOME PLANS

You've scanned the space, so you already know which areas are crying out for help. You could start with the loudest one right now if the caffeine has kicked in and you're feeling motivated. Or you could start with the one quietly clearing its throat and build momentum. But don't feel bad if you're sitting on your bed, frozen in stunned panic and listening to screams from every direction. It's a lot of stuff. What you need is a plan of attack.

Don't be scared off by the word *plan*. I'm not asking you to break out the project-management software or whip up a PowerPoint presentation. (If that's your thing, though, go for it. I'm a sucker for a pretty spreadsheet.) Just start putting your thoughts into some sort of recognizable order. Feeling overwhelmed? Try a brain dump. Uninspiring name aside, brain dumps can be really helpful for corralling the chaos of your mind. The concept is simple: grab a piece of paper or a notebook and scribble down everything clutter related that's been swirling around in your mind. Some things to include are:

- The spots you want to work on and why
- The things you already know you want gone and where they might go

LEARN HOW TO CORRAL THE CHAOS

- The things you might want to sell (we'll decide later whether that's worth the effort)

It doesn't have to be neat and tidy at first. Once you get everything down on paper, you can start organizing things into a checklist, a plan of action, a murder board, or a gaggle of sticky notes. Personally, I love a list, but do what works for your particular brain chemistry.

CHOOSE YOUR OWN ADVENTURE

Much like that too-tight blanket hoodie you bought off a discount site that only Santa's elves would call "oversize," decluttering styles aren't one-size-fits-all. What works for your type-A friend whose dorm room was always tidy might not work for you if you majored in procrastination. If you're living with chronic illness, you might need to work in sprints or take advantage of good days with a decluttering marathon. You might be neurospicy and loathe to put things away for fear of forgetting they exist. (It's me, hi!) I can't speak to your situation, but I can give you a bunch of tools to try until you find what works for you. Just don't count them out if they're not a good fit on the first try—what you deem helpful can change depending on the day and whether you've recently had a nap. The important thing isn't *how* you declutter. It's *that* you declutter. The goal is the same no matter what: to carve out a home you love without leaving a mess for anyone else to clean up.

TIPS FOR OVERTHINKERS

Even people who aren't traditionally overthinkers—the kinds of people who might buy a timeshare on a whim or try gas-station sushi—become overthinkers when it comes to getting rid of their stuff. So don't skip this section just because you don't usually agonize over decisions. These tips can help you get past all the excuses that stand between you and the thrift store.

Do you love it, or are you just used to it?

TRY THE FIVE-SECOND APPROACH

Challenge yourself to make a decision about each piece in under five seconds. This approach presumes that you actually already know what you want to do, but guilt or fear or conditioning is keeping you from doing it. Five seconds is just enough time to ask yourself whether you need the thing, use the thing, or love the thing and get an instinctive reaction without any equivocation or debate. Let your gut do the talking, then listen. And don't let those outside factors worm their way back in. You can even count down out loud or set a timer to give yourself that push to beat the clock. You'll start to feel a sense of urgency, which activates your unconscious mind, and you'll suddenly know what you want. The real trick is not talking yourself out of the decision after you've made it.

RATE YOUR STUFF

When you're on the fence about an object, try rating it. On a scale of one to ten, how much do you want to keep that monkey lamp? (No adding points for nostalgia.) If it's a five or below, you can probably let it go. If it's a six or seven, ask yourself why it's not a ten. Do you love it, or are you just used to it? And if it's an eight or higher, congratulations, you've found something worth keeping. This little rating system helps cut through the emotional noise and makes decision-making a whole lot easier.

DO THE MATH

Sometimes, leaning into the overthinking can be helpful— for example, doing the actual math on how much money your stuff is costing you by sitting around unused. Unless

> ### ⸺ DON'T GET DISCOURAGED ⸺
> When you think about it, we're all just birds feathering our nests. Each twig, leaf, and clump of pet hair woven into it holds meaning. It might be a symbol of our hard work or something we once needed, or it could just be a really pretty feather. Of course, it's going to be hard to remove things from your nest. It's counterintuitive. But it does get easier. And after a while, you'll start to love how spacious your home feels without that excess fluff. Keep going, little bird.

you live totally off the grid, you're paying for the space you occupy. Divide how much you pay each month by the number of square feet you rent or own and you'll get how much each square foot costs you. Let's say that chair full of laundry in the corner of your bedroom takes up 9 square feet. With today's rent prices, that little corner might be costing you $15 or more *per month*. Does a chair-shaped laundry basket feel like a good use of your money? Or would you rather learn how to put away your clothes like an adult and let that chair pay its rent as a reading nook?

ENLIST THE HELP OF A DECISIVE FRIEND

Not everyone is built for decluttering. The sibling who can't decide between hot dogs and hamburgers at the cookout?

Not your guy. The parent who mewls every time you try to trash tchotchkes from your childhood? Absolutely not. The friend who orders food for the group when everyone's annoyingly hemming and hawing at the menu? That person has potential. Bare minimum: you want someone who's supportive, strong-minded, and has absolutely no skin in this game other than wanting you to thrive.

Create some breathing room around the stuff you truly value.

IMAGINE YOU HAVE AN HOUR TO PACK

If you knew you only had an hour to pack and couldn't come back, what would you take with you? Not to get too doom-and-gloom here, but with natural disasters on the rise, this scenario is not totally unrealistic. Too many people have lived it. But it can certainly help clarify what's *really* important to you because you don't have time to factor in guilt, conditioning, or pride. Don't spend more than a few minutes thinking about it—just pay attention to your first impulses. What items spring to mind as absolutely-must-keeps? Maybe an album full of cherished photos? The necklace your grandmother gave you? A few favorite decor items? As you do this exercise, you're also going to notice things that are an immediate nope. Don't even think about keeping those things. Instead, create some breathing room around the stuff you truly value.

TIPS FOR PROCRASTINATORS

Hello, my like-minded friends! People procrastinate for a lot of reasons. Sure, laziness is one of those reasons, but it's not the most common one. Overwhelm and dread are certainly up there. Sometimes, procrastination is perfectionism in disguise—you worry you can't do something perfectly, so you don't even want to try. Some people procrastinate to regain a sense of control. Others struggle with executive function or time management. Our brains are weird and wonderful and sometimes entirely unhelpful. Regardless of your reasons for putting things off, these tips can help. You know what's *not* going to help? Saying you'll get around to it. You won't. Pick a tip and get to work.

TRY THE FIVE-MINUTE APPROACH

Set a timer for five minutes and challenge yourself to declutter whatever you can in that time. The toughest thing for procrastinators is just getting started, especially

LEARN HOW TO CORRAL THE CHAOS   53

with a large, time-consuming task like decluttering. Knowing you're only going to do five minutes takes the pressure off. Once you get started, you probably won't want to stop. But if all you do is that five minutes of decluttering, it's still better than nothing. Want to do more? Set the timer for twenty minutes, or even an hour. Just don't get too ambitious. The point is to trick yourself into decluttering, not talk yourself out of it by turning it into a chore.

START SO, SO SMALL

Another way to take the pressure off is to start with a single, tiny task. Breaking things down into smaller (even microscopic) steps can help you outsmart overwhelm. So declutter a pencil cup or the box where you keep the cough drops. Declutter only your tank tops, then move on to your tees, then go through your sweaters. Most importantly, start with stuff that doesn't matter—old

> ### ⋛ PUT THE PHONE AWAY ⋚
> Hot tip for anyone who's easily distracted: use a kitchen timer instead of your phone. Don't give yourself an opportunity to start scrolling. In fact, you should probably hide the phone from yourself. In another room. The temptation is just too strong for us.

appliance manuals, stained food containers, pens you've accidentally stolen from restaurants (why would you hold on to the evidence?). We're going to build up to the sentimental stuff. For now, you just want to start building the habit of decluttering, and that means racking up some easy wins. But again, once you get started, you'll probably feel so accomplished that you won't want to stop.

> *You just want to start building the habit of decluttering.*

DECLUTTER LIKE YOU'RE MOVING

While being forced to declutter on a clock is a level of angst no one needs, some people do benefit from a little anxiety when trying to get stuff done. If you do your best cleaning right before house guests come, this method is probably for you. Set your "move-out date" and try to get a good chunk done by that deadline. (Make sure it's a Goldilocks date—not so far away that it saps your motivation, but not so soon that it leaves you huddled in a heap of despair amid piles of clothes.) On top of that, adopt a moving mindset. Ask yourself whether you can really be bothered to pack, haul, and unpack items you're on the fence about. If the answer is no, those items can probably go. If it's yes, you know they're keepers.

TIPS FOR STRUCTURE LOVERS

If you're the type of person who thrives on schedules, systems, and a solid game plan, you've probably already mapped out your decluttering strategy. But that doesn't mean you won't occasionally get stuck in the muck of it all. Clutter is like a toddler—unpredictable. You could be the best parent in the world, and your toddler will still find new ways to humble you. But these tips can help you wrest back control.

TAKE BREAKS

Breaks are essential for every kind of declutterer, but they're a must for procrastinators. When you feel like you've hit a wall, walk away. Get a snack, do some doomscrolling, have a nap—whatever helps you feel like you're in control of your time or gives you the hit of dopamine you need to keep going. Then declutter one more thing. If you get stuck on a particular item, unsure of which pile to put it in, move on to something else. There's no point in torturing yourself. In fact, it's a good way to end up feeling burned out and resentful. Give yourself what you need to get the job done.

USE TIME BLOCKING

Time blocking is a simple but powerful way to structure your decluttering sessions. Instead of vaguely planning to "clean out the garage someday," you commit to a specific amount of time on specific days and add it to your calendar, just like you would a work meeting or a dentist appointment. If you really want to be detailed about it, you can set tasks for that time (e.g., half an hour to clean out the bathroom cabinet). The beauty of time blocking is that it removes decision fatigue. When the time arrives, you don't have to think about where to start or how long to keep going. You just show up and do the thing.

By making those small, consistent decisions, you form a sustainable decluttering habit.

MAKE IT A HABIT

You don't need to have a dedicated decluttering session to get rid of a torn shirt or a lotion that didn't work for you. At some point, ditching those kinds of things will become second nature. Until then, you could challenge yourself to find three things to declutter every day, or every week— whatever feels reasonable to you. You could start with three per week and build up to three per day. By making those small, consistent decisions, you form a sustainable decluttering habit.

If you set the bar at perfection, you're guaranteed to hit your head on it.

TRY BODY DOUBLING

Decluttering with a friend who dishes out tough love is great, but just having another human in the room has been proven to help people stay focused. Body doubling works by holding you accountable to someone else, keeping you engaged, and making decluttering feel less isolating. (Let's be honest, you're a lot less likely to spend an hour on your phone with someone watching.) You just need someone who will go about their business while you go about yours. This is the opposite of inviting over an opinionated friend, although they're welcome if they can sit quietly until they're expressly asked for help. Having someone around who will gently (or not-so-gently) remind you that you don't need six identical black cardigans isn't the worst thing for your productivity.

TIPS FOR PERFECTIONISTS

Don't get caught in the trap of thinking you have to do this thing at 100 percent if you're going to do it at all. We're not aiming for perfection (which, as it so happens, is an unattainable construct fed to us by TV shows and musty Madison Avenue copywriters). We're aiming for progress. Five minutes here and there adds up. One or two items rehomed at a time adds up. Little by little, you'll create a space you love and a sense of freedom—from obligation, from generational clutter, *and* from the lure of those crafty salespeople. That beats perfection any day. Still having trouble getting started? Try these tips.

AIM LOWER

If you set the bar at perfection, you're guaranteed to hit your head on it. You need to be realistic. Going from dopamine decor (surrounding yourself with odd, colorful little things you love) to full minimalist is not realistic. Having a home that always looks like an upscale home-decor store is not realistic. And if you're honest with yourself, you'll discover you weren't even the one who set the bar that high—maybe it was your overly critical mom or an annoyingly perky influencer, but it wasn't you. I'm going to let you in on a little secret: when it comes to your decluttering situation, you get to decide what "perfect" is. Your home should work for you and the way you live (as a normal human who sometimes forgets to put their boxers in the hamper).

DO YOUR BEST

A lot of perfectionists push themselves past their breaking point to meet those unrealistic expectations, and they feel they've failed if they fall short. But there's a helpful saying: If all you have to give is 40 percent, and you give it, you've given 100 percent. And in case you didn't know,

⁂TOSS YOUR BUYER'S REMORSE⁂

Perfectionists are especially prone to letting buyer's remorse get in the way of letting go. So you spent good money on that fancy cast-iron cookware. If you can't be bothered to haul it out of the cupboard to use it, it shouldn't be taking up space there. The money is already gone—there's no point in beating yourself up over it. You had good intentions; it just didn't work out like you thought it would. Are you trying to teach yourself a lesson by letting it continue to live in your home and haunt you like the Ghost of Bad Purchases past? You deserve better than that. Learn the lesson, let the stuff go, and move on.

clutter is morally neutral—you're not a better person if your house looks like a magazine cover, just like you're not a bad person if it's gotten away from you. Just do your best, whatever your best looks like each day.

DO IT ANYWAY

The best thing you can do for your perfectionist self is accept that, no matter how reasonable or lofty a goal you set for yourself, you may never reach it. Declutter anyway. Take small steps toward your goals. Making progress is better than preemptively proclaiming defeat and settling in for a bingefest of *The Office*. Actually, bingeing something fun *while* you declutter can be a great way to distract yourself from worrying about it.

TIPS FOR VISUAL LEARNERS

A lot of the tips we've covered so far are designed to help you get out of your head or overcome certain habits and emotions. But sometimes, you just need a good physical reminder of what you're trying to do here. Seeing your progress—or the full expanse of your clutter—laid out in front of you can make a huge difference. And getting clear on which items turn you into a heart-eyes emoji can make it easy to ditch those that pale in comparison.

LEARN HOW TO CORRAL THE CHAOS

TAKE BEFORE AND AFTER PICS

I have a terrible habit of forgetting to take pictures of what things looked like before a decluttering project. The finished product feels great, but it would feel better if I could see how far the space had come. (Entire home-improvement networks were created based on this fact.) So don't be like me—snap some pics right now of the spaces you hope to tackle. Take more as you work through your project. Then, when you're finished, you can sit back and see what a dramatic difference your efforts are making. Few things are more motivating. If you're someone who finds accountability (or the threat of shame) even more rousing, post your before and during shots publicly. Then rake in the praise with your afters.

CHOOSE YOUR YARDSTICK

Find one item that represents everything a keeper should be: you love it beyond reason, you use it all the time, you consider it essential. Pull it out and put it in plain view while you declutter. That's your yardstick. That's the thing you measure everything else against. You could even go a step further and pull out something that represents everything a keeper *shouldn't* be: you're hanging on to it "just in case," you're saving it for someone else, you feel

> ### ⧽WHAT IF IT HAD POOP ON IT?⧼
>
> I'm constantly learning new decluttering tips from social media, and this has to be one of my favorites. If you're hemming and hawing about an object, ask yourself what you would do if it had poop on it. Would you clean it? Or would you throw it away? If it's not worth cleaning, it's probably not worth keeping.

guilty getting rid of it. Make sure it's something you really want to get rid of. The point of both yardsticks is to help you make quick decisions, not to help you amass a pile of stuff you're equally on the fence about.

TIPS FOR EVERYONE

Hopefully some of the tips so far have inspired you to get moving, or at least piqued your curiosity. If you haven't found anything that speaks to you, don't worry. One thing about decluttering: there are endless ways to do it. And here are a few more with universal appeal.

LET YOUR PRIORITIES CHANGE

Give yourself permission to let go of the things that no longer align with your life. The things you valued ten years ago aren't necessarily the things you value now. It's OK to let go of those past priorities and make room

LEARN HOW TO CORRAL THE CHAOS

for what actually matters to you today. Maybe you used to be really into scrapbooking, but now your supplies are gathering dust while you spend your free time hiking. Or maybe you swore you'd get back into playing the guitar, but yours is sitting in the basement untouched. Decluttering isn't just about getting rid of stuff—it's also about making space for the things that matter to you now.

Decluttering isn't just about getting rid of stuff—it's also about making space for the things that matter to you now.

WORK UP TO THE SENTIMENTAL STUFF

As you declutter other things, you'll inevitably come across something that stirs up memories. Do not go down the rabbit hole. Next thing you know, three hours will have gone by, and you'll have nothing to show for it except a pair of glittery Y2K New Year's Eve novelty glasses newly obscuring your view. Anything that threatens to jettison your momentum needs to wait until you're deep in an "I don't need this stuff" mindset.

USE IT OR LOSE IT

We often think "this is just what I need" when we buy new things. You're sure you'll use that portable blender all the time. And then you shove a toaster pastry in your mouth on your way out the door while that blender remains in the cupboard and a bag of spinach wilts in the back of your fridge. But some day, you might fundamentally change who you are as a person, right? No, you won't. Lean into who you are now—it makes becoming a better version of you infinitely easier. For example, you could make a sweet-yet-healthy breakfast that lets you grab and go, like overnight oats, and offer the blender to that friend who (bafflingly) gets up before dawn to jog every morning. Be prepared to accept no for an answer and donate it, though. Death cleaning means not forcing your stuff on other people.

Lean into who you are now—it makes becoming a better version of you infinitely easier.

DECLUTTER SEASONALLY

Conventional wisdom tells you to declutter your closets seasonally. "If you've gone a whole winter without wearing that heavy knit sweater, it might be time to let it go," they say. It's sound advice, but don't stop there. You can use seasonal decluttering on a lot more than clothes. If you've gone a whole winter without using that tanning lotion you bought to combat your ghostly pallor or a whole summer without breaking out the pool noodles, it might be time to send *those* things packing. (Unless you want to test your luck by trying that opened lotion next year. But I'd start with a *really* inconspicuous area.)

DON'T LET HIDDEN STUFF SUCK YOU IN

That fondue set you found in the back of the closet? If you didn't know you had it, you definitely don't need it. You might find yourself thinking, "I wish I'd had that for my dinner party . . ." But you didn't, and you lived. You

> #### ⋝KEEP GOING⋜
>
> There's going to come a time—actually, it's going to happen a lot—when you want to give in to the resistance you're feeling. You're sick of decluttering. It's too hard. You feel guilty about all the stuff you have that you don't use, or all the stuff you're getting rid of. You just don't want to do it anymore. It's understandable. This process can take a lot out of you. But you have to move through those feelings.

went with a beautiful charcuterie board and your dinner party was a hit. So again I say, you don't need it. Don't let that little lightning strike of dopamine you get when you rediscover something trick you into keeping it.

Seeing a clear or cleanly decorated flat surface is good for our brains.

CLEAR THE CLUTTER MAGNETS

Don't forget about those areas that seem to attract random clutter. The treadmill and the chair in the corner both invite the hanging of not-quite-dirty laundry for some reason. And think about all the crap that ends up on tables (dining, entryway, coffee, side) and nightstands (which are basically tables with drawers). Seeing a clear or cleanly decorated flat surface is good for our brains—it actually reduces anxiety and boosts focus. But if you have extra clutter and zero organizational systems, both your surfaces and your mental health suffer.

You don't need to break out the label maker and colored bins to solve this problem. Instead, create small systems that work for the way you live. Give the not-quite-dirty laundry its own hamper, put a little basket for keys and sunglasses on the entryway table, and spend five minutes a day doing a sweep of your home and putting stuff where it actually belongs. Simply paying attention to where things tend to end up and making a real home for them there can make all the difference.

HUSH THE SPACE

Ever notice how a room feels different after you clear off a cluttered surface? That's the magic of hushing the space—removing excess visual noise so your brain can finally relax. When you're in the thick of decluttering, it can be hard to tell what actually matters to you because everything blends into one overwhelming mess. The solution? Take everything out. Strip the space down to its bare bones and sit with it for a moment. Breathe. Then, put back only what you truly love, use, or need.

You'll be amazed at how quickly you realize some things were never necessary to your happiness. That decorative bowl you kept out of obligation? The three-wick candles you forgot you even had? If it isn't adding to the calm, it's adding to the chaos. Hushing the space lets you reset, making it clear what deserves a place in your home, and what was just taking up space.

Knowing that something has served you well can help you let go of it when you're tempted to hang on too long.

TAKE A MOMENT TO BE GRATEFUL

If you do it right (which is to say, mindfully and not like you're on some sort of competitive reality show), decluttering can steep you in gratitude. It's an opportunity to see how far you've come, to appreciate all the little things that make up your life, and to revel in the memories you've created around them. As you decide certain items no longer fit into your life, take a moment to sit with that gratitude. Not only is it good for your mental and emotional health, but knowing that something has served you well can also help you let go of it when you're tempted to hang on too long.

WATCH OUT FOR ASPIRATIONAL CLUTTER

You buy a pretty planner every January thinking you're going to be the most organized person on earth. You get a pricey walking pad and swear you'll hop on every day. You buy bento boxes to meal prep. And then you flake.

It's not your fault—you had the best intentions. That stuff just wasn't right for you. But now that you have it, you have to avoid the pitfall of keeping it just so you won't feel like a failure. I have bad news for you: walking past that walking pad on your way to the couch every day isn't going to do much to assuage your guilt. It's good to have goals. But if you notice you've fallen into certain patterns over the years—like leaving those pretty planners blank— take a beat. Think about what really works for you, what's realistic for your lifestyle. Then see if there are ways to gauge whether a new purchase is necessary.

DO THIS FOR YOU

Here's my best advice: If you haven't already, now is the time to dig in. You have to want to do this. You have to make the commitment—to yourself, to your happiness, and to the future you're creating—to do this thing. This isn't about the physical work or turning decluttering into your full-time job. This is about being mentally and emotionally ready to transform your life. If you feel resentful (or just tired on an existential level), return to the motivation you found in chapter 2. Take a breather if you need it. (You'll be back the next time you trip over your shoes, bump into your entryway table, and knock a junk drawer's worth of receipts, loose change, mail, broken sunglasses, and dead batteries onto the floor.) Take a step back and remember that, although death cleaning will benefit your loved ones too, you're really doing this for you. Make the choice to go all-in, then hold yourself accountable.

≡ TAKE ACTION

If you learn anything from this chapter, hopefully it's that decluttering doesn't have to be a grand event. Small, intentional steps add up fast. Here's how to get the ball rolling:

- **COMMIT.** Whatever else you do, make a commitment right now that you're going to see this thing through.

- **PICK A TIP.** Which tip makes this death-cleaning thing feel doable? Start there. Put it to good use.

- **BREATHE.** I know, I've said this one before. But once you're in the thick of things, you might forget. Deep breaths are magic. They can help you calm down, stay motivated, and make decisions.

NOW, TACKLE THE CLOSET

ACTUALLY, YOU CAN DECLUTTER IN WHATEVER ORDER WORKS FOR YOU—with one caveat. Save the sentimental stuff for last. If you start flipping through old concert tees and movie ticket stubs now, you'll look up and realize you've lost an hour (or five) going down memory lane with nothing to show for it. But personally, I like to start with the bedroom. Bedroom closets are where good intentions go to die. Clothes you swore you'd wear, a surf shop's worth of flip-flops, enough luggage for a family of ten, and random collections of clutter that wouldn't fit anywhere else—it's all in there. Someday, you'll try to shove in one more purse and the whole thing will explode. And your closet's not alone. From your dressers and nightstands to the space under your bed, it's all full to bursting. Let's fix that, once and for all.

When you let go of excuses, you can end up with a closet full of pieces you love.

START WITH YOUR CLOTHES

The things taking up the most space in your brain and your bedroom are your clothes. Thanks to fast fashion, one-click shopping, and eerily accurate targeted ads, they add up faster than almost anything else in our homes. (Except maybe kitchen gadgets. Who can resist a miniature waffle maker with a snowman plate?) It's time to face the fabric jungle. If it doesn't fit, flatter, or make sense for your life *now*, why are you keeping it? Just in case? You know by now that's not a valid reason for something to be living rent-free in your home. When you let go of excuses, you can end up with a closet full of pieces you love. (And probably a dresser, too. We're not going for minimalism here.)

FIND YOUR YARDSTICK

We covered this in the last chapter, but in case you need a refresher: a yardstick is a definite keeper. It's something you love, use, and need—in this case, the holy grail of clothing items. And you're going to measure everything else against it to help you make quick and easy decisions. So, start by finding your yardstick. Hang it somewhere you can see it (and where it won't get mixed into the chaos I'm about to inflict on you).

EMPTY YOUR CLOSET

Piling up every piece of clothing you own may feel extreme, but it's the fastest way to declutter your wardrobe. Empty your closet, drawers, and any storage bins hiding under your bed onto a clean, flat surface, such as said bed. (Just make sure you have plenty of time or somewhere else to sleep that night.) Pull from the pile any pieces that you immediately know measure up to your yardstick piece—these should be your absolute favorites, the ones you wear constantly, the ones they'll have to pry from your cold, dead hands. (Too far?) Hang those in your closet, even if that's not where they usually go. The goal is to see your favorite pieces all together. These will form the basis of your new wardrobe. The following sections will help you build around these core pieces, filling in any gaps from your clutter pile.

It's time to start fresh and take control of your closet.

DEFINE YOUR STYLE

Most closets are more like chaotic time capsules of their owners' taste over decades. On top of the everyday items that have cycled in through countless trends, there are the "I might need this" outfits, the on-sale impulse buys, and the "one day I'll be fancy" wild cards. And yet we still struggle to find something to wear. It's time to start fresh and take control of your closet. You'll begin by defining your style—your *real* style, not the style of the person you think you should be. A closet full of suits isn't going to do you any good if you work from home in sweats every day and like it that way.

You've already started the process by pulling together the pieces you love most. What do they say about your

> **THE DEATH-CLEANING CONNECTION**
>
> You might be asking yourself, "What does this have to do with death cleaning?" Honestly? Not much. This part (much like this whole death-cleaning thing) is primarily for you. It's so you can live out your life wearing things you love and not wasting time deciding between nearly identical shirts. But if you want to zoom out, think of it this way: the less excess you have, the less mess you leave behind for your loved ones to worry about. And if they want to keep something from your closet, it's nice to know they'll be picking from your favorites.

style? Is it casual? Boho? Sophisticated? Use your style as a guide as you dig through your clutter pile. Are there any other pieces still in there that would feel right at home? (Don't add anything back in you were on the fence about or ready to toss.) Are there any that definitely wouldn't fit in? It's OK to keep pieces that don't necessarily jibe with each other. But seeing a small collection of your favorites should give you some much-needed perspective on the others.

LEAVE YOURSELF SOME OPTIONS

A perfectly curated capsule wardrobe is great in theory. A small, manageable number of pieces that all work together perfectly because they're all in the same color family? It would certainly cut down on your morning rush. But it's not very realistic for the way most people live. We want variety. We want options. And yes, we also need a few basics we can mix and match. (That white tee may not be bringing you joy now, but it will when you have nothing to pair with those teal pants you love.) We just don't need five old pairs of jeans that don't fit or a jacket we only keep because it was expensive.

The goal here isn't to strip your wardrobe down to the bare bones—it's to make sure what you own actually serves you. So, looking through your clutter pile, are there any pieces you need to make your core wardrobe work? Are there any pieces you just want, even if it doesn't really make sense?

If something hasn't earned a spot in your regular rotation, it's time to let it go.

NOTICE YOUR HABITS

You've probably heard of the 80/20 rule—it's the idea that 80 percent of your results come from just 20 percent of your efforts. Well, the same logic applies to your wardrobe: you wear 20 percent of your clothes 80 percent

> ### ⊱SHOP INTENTIONALLY⊰
> If you're not crazy about one of those basics you saved, donate it and keep an eye out for something you like better. You don't want to shop just to shop (that's how we got here in the first place), but shopping with intention can actually help you keep clutter at bay. You're less likely to settle for something that's "meh" that will end up in the donate pile six months from now.

of the time. The other 80 percent? It's just sitting there, looking pretty, taking up space, and silently judging you every time you reach past it.

What's in your neglected 80 percent? Which pieces never make it out of the drawer or closet? Are you hanging on to outfits for a fantasy version of yourself—the one who wears ties to work or actually enjoys high heels? Are you saving things for a special occasion that never seems to come? Or do you just have items that, for some reason, never feel quite right? Whatever the case, if something hasn't earned a spot in your regular rotation, it's time to let it go. Future You will be thrilled on some frantic morning, when getting dressed is 80 percent less stressful.

USE THE SEASONS

The easiest way to keep your wardrobe under control is to check in with it regularly, and the changing seasons give you the perfect excuse. When the weather shifts, take a moment to reassess your clothing. Did you go the entire winter without touching that wool coat? Did summer pass without you once reaching for that strappy sundress? If you didn't wear something all season, chances are good you won't next year either. And checking in quarterly helps you avoid having to create another clutter pile like the one now occupying the entirety of your bed. For now, just think back to last season and consider tossing the items in your pile that didn't make an appearance.

GIVE UP ON LOST SOCKS

I know firsthand the pain of losing a favorite sock. But after a few months, it's time to give up the ghost and toss the remaining sock. (That is, unless you have the ability and desire to scope the washer and dryer vents.) This goes for anything with unrepairable holes and unfixable stains—and/or holes or stains you can't be bothered to fix. It also goes for anything that doesn't fit or feel good on. It doesn't matter how cute that mock turtleneck is if you can't stand the feel of fabric against your neck. You're either never going to wear it or you're going to be miserable when you do. If you haven't fit into those jeans in five years, you're going to feel bad every time you look at them. What's the point? Invest in clothes that work for who you are and let the rest go. (I know, I sound like a broken record. But some people need to hear it again.)

DON'T TORTURE YOURSELF

If you're on the fence about a piece of clothing, you can probably let it go. Why are you hanging on to it? Because you're worried you might regret it some far-off day? That's fair, but I promise, it's mostly unfounded. More often than

RECYCLE THOSE SPARES

Clothing items that aren't fit to donate don't need to end up in the trash. (Except for soiled clothing, which should go straight in the bin.) Search for clothing recyclers near you and online who will process and upcycle those threadbare tees. Fast fashion has created a massive environmental crisis, with tens of billions of pounds of textile waste ending up in landfills each year. Taking a few extra seconds to unload your unwanted clothes responsibly is a much better legacy than adding to the problem.

not, you won't even remember the stuff you got rid of once it's gone. Out of sight, out of mind (just like it's been at the back of your closet for the last five years).

It gets easier from here on out. Decluttering pieces that don't serve you will become a habit.

Are there pieces I wish I hadn't gotten rid of? Sure. I see a shirt in an old picture and get wistful from time to time. Then I remember why I got rid of it—it had an unrepairable hole, it was tissue-paper thin after 500 washes, it didn't fit as well as it used to, or I just never wore it anymore. In other words, you're not tossing these items for no good reason. Just make sure you've checked all the pockets on a piece before giving it away. You won't regret donating that old winter coat, but you will be sorry if you send your credit card with it.

ORGANIZE WHAT'S LEFT

Now that you've decluttered your clothes, feel free to put them wherever you need them. Those sweaters that "grow" when left on hangers? Give them the coveted drawer space. And if you find yourself still struggling to close your dresser drawers, don't panic. This first pass

> ### ⸱PUT A BIN IN THE CLOSET⸱
> The best way to declutter? Make it too easy not to. I maintain that just putting things in pretty bins solves nothing. But keeping a bin, a trash bag, or even a Chewy box in your closet can help you declutter whenever the mood strikes. As you're getting ready in the morning, you notice you skip over a top you haven't worn in ages and casually toss it in the bin. Once the bin is full, it can—and should—go straight to the thrift store (or wherever you prefer to donate).

gave you a fresh start. As long as you don't take it as tacit permission to go on a shopping spree, it gets easier from here on out. Decluttering pieces that don't serve you will become a habit. And little by little, those drawers will feel lighter.

WHITTLE DOWN THE REST OF YOUR WARDROBE

Now that you've got your clothing sorted, you can move on to the other items that will make up your newly refreshed wardrobe. You've already done the heavy lifting—you've defined your style and set the bar for favorites. Figuring out which shoes and belts complement what's left should be a breeze. (Compared to starting from scratch, anyway. You'll still have to overcome the stranglehold your excuses have on you.)

YOUR SHOE COLLECTION

Most people have way more pairs of shoes than they actually wear (a perfect example of the 80/20 rule). How many pairs do you really need? How many are sitting in your closet, by your front door, and under your bed, untouched and waiting for the right occasion? Be honest—do you really need those blister-inducing heels or those sneakers you keep meaning to break in but never do? The best shoes feel comfy right away. If a pair makes you walk like a newborn deer, it's not worth keeping. Neither is any pair that's falling apart or has holes in its soles, no matter how much you once loved them. Stick with the shoes you actually wear, and let go of the ones that are just taking up space. Your closet and your feet will thank you.

BAGS OF ALL KINDS

You can never have too many bags, right? Wrong. Too much of a good thing is still too much. As it was with shoes, it should be simpler to whittle down your purse collection once you've chosen your clothing. Ditch any

⸱REPLACE THE THINGS THAT MATTER⸱

Are you truly sad to say goodbye to a well-loved piece of clothing or pair of shoes? As long as it's not one-of-a-kind, I have good news for you: secondhand sales have never been more popular or accessible. You can probably replace that item with one that's exactly the same and in better shape for a very reasonable price. The aim of decluttering isn't to live like a miser or a monk; the aim is to love and use the things you have. If you love those blush-colored patent pumps you don't wear anymore because you've scuffed them into oblivion, toss the old ones and invest in a new or more gently used pair. (Also invest in some leather cleaner.)

purse that doesn't complement your chosen style (or make you so happy you don't care). But laptop bags, totes, and backpacks are trickier. Luggage and duffels get an honorable mention here, too. They're not beholden to your wardrobe, and they tend to multiply when you're not looking. You find a new one you love and add it to your stockpile instead of doing the responsible thing and getting rid of an old one. And each bag contains its own assortment of crumpled receipts, dried-out pens, lip balms, toothpaste, and who knows what else, multiplying the odds of you losing among them something you actually need, like your insurance cards. If you've got more bags than occasions to use them, it's time to pare down. Just make sure you go through every nook and cranny before you give them up.

Too much of a good thing is still too much.

ACCESSORIES

When is the last time you wore a belt? If you can't remember, maybe you don't need five of them. Obviously, this advice is not belt specific. Apply it to whatever it is that lives in your closet unused for months or years at a time—scarves, hats, sunglasses, mittens, and fuzzy slippers included. I know you love those slippers. But do you actually wear them? No, because they don't stay on your feet. Fuzzy socks are easier and warmer. I don't have to tell you what to do. You already know. But if it makes you feel better, just imagine how cozy those slippers will make someone else. (Presumably, someone with wider feet.)

JEWELRY

Some people have a vast collection of jewelry that they meticulously match to their outfits. Some break out the heirloom pieces for special occasions. Most people can't be bothered to take off their jewelry and just wear the same pieces until they break or wear down beyond repair. (Don't mind me sheepishly raising my own hand here.) Meanwhile, the rest of their jewelry sits untouched and tarnishing in a box or a drawer. If you fall in camps one or two, no notes. If you fall into that third camp like I do, it's time to get to work.

The fact that jewelry takes up relatively little space does not absolve you of having to deal with it like the rest of the clutter in your home. Ask yourself the same questions you do with anything else: Which pieces do

> ### ≳MAKE SOME EXTRA CASH≲
>
> Although you can sell unwanted pieces at local jewelers, gold stores, and pawn shops, you might get more buck for your bang using online resellers, especially if your jewelry comes from well-known brands. And auction sites aren't the only options. Poshmark, a site that sprang up as a clothing reseller, now lets you sell all sorts of items—jewelry, purses, shoes, home decor, and more. But remember this: your stuff is only worth what someone else is willing to pay, and it may take a while to sell. Do you really want to hang on to those nautical cufflinks for who-knows-how-long if you'll only make twenty bucks off them? You have to decide what your limits are.

you love? Which pieces are you over? Which pieces are you hanging on to "just in case"? Which ones do you feel guilty getting rid of? We're not doing excuses anymore, remember? Anything you don't love and use goes. Ask your friends and family whether there are any pieces they'd like to have—especially if they're heirlooms. If they say no, then sell or donate them. Opening your jewelry box to find a small collection of things you love feels like a breath of fresh, guilt-free air.

WRANGLE THE REST OF YOUR CLOSET

We all know that clothes and shoes aren't the only things taking up space in your bedroom closet. Throw blankets, photo albums, keepsakes, storage bins you've yet to use, and mystery bins full of forgotten odds and ends have a way of piling up. To really finish decluttering your closet, you'll need to go through those. Breathe—you don't have to go through them now. But, if you have some space to spare, do yourself a favor and take all that extra stuff out of your closet. Ideally, put it in another room. Then look at your closet without it. It looks incredible, right? All of your hard work is on display, and you can actually feel the difference.

Remember that feeling when you do go through the rest of your closet-dwelling clutter. And know this: just because you *can* store something in your closet doesn't mean you should. Embrace the open space. Give your things some breathing room, especially now that you've gone to all the trouble of paring down the excess.

Embrace the open space.

As for what's left? Do exactly what you've been doing. Go through and look at each item. Ask yourself whether it's earning its keep. If it's something that tugs on your heartstrings or might benefit someone else, put it aside until you get to chapter 9. But those storage bins you bought during previous (failed) attempts at decluttering and still haven't found a use for? Out they go.

THE BEDROOM AT LARGE

Once you've recovered from decluttering your closet, you can work on the other areas of your bedroom that tend to accumulate clutter: your nightstands and under your bed. Bedrooms should be restful, not a storage unit disguised as a sleeping area. And a nightstand should be a functional little oasis, not a junk drawer with a lamp on

> ### ⋛GOOD ENERGY⋚
>
> A clutter-free bedroom isn't just nice to look at—it can actually improve your sleep and overall well-being. Feng shui principles suggest that you should keep pathways clear so energy (and, you know, *you*) can flow freely. Avoid storing things under the bed—trapped clutter can lead to trapped stress. And if your nightstand looks like a garage sale, tidy it up. Going to bed in a calm space means you'll wake up feeling refreshed instead of tangled in last night's anxiety dreams.

top. Clear out the tangled cords, expired moisturizers, and to-do lists from three years ago. Keep only the essentials— bonus points if they actually help you wind down at night.

If you're using the space under your bed for storage, be intentional about it. Storing out-of-season clothing under there is fine, as long as you've gone through it. Storing a random smattering of stuff you haven't had have time to deal with, not so much. Deal with it now. If you haven't checked what's under there in years, it's probably not important enough to keep.

THE OTHER CLOSETS

Your bedroom closet isn't the only one brimming with stuff you don't need. Closets are like black holes for clutter. Except, unlike black holes, they have limits. So they swallow up more and more of your stuff until, one day, you open a door and get taken out by an avalanche of winter coats and expired sunscreen. Before we move on, let's deal with those black holes.

THE HALL CLOSET

Coats, umbrellas, snow gear, sports gear—your hall closet is doing a lot of heavy lifting. And you probably couldn't name half of what's in there without looking. If you're holding on to every jacket you've owned since high school, let some go. Keep the ones you actually wear and donate the ones you don't. The puffer jacket that makes you look like a marshmallow and feel like a sauna? Unless it's your winter MVP, say goodbye. Umbrellas are another sneaky

⋝YOU CAN'T FIGHT PROGRESS⋜

Stop fighting with fitted sheets that were made for old mattresses. The days of box springs and 10-inch mattresses are gone. If you've upgraded your bed in the last few years, you need fitted sheets with deep pockets—14 to 18 inches—for those three extra layers of memory foam under your back. Donate your old sheet sets and invest in some made for modern mattresses.

culprit. Do you need five? Probably not. Keep a small one for your bag, a good one for your car, and *maybe* a backup. The rest can go. And let's not forget the sports gear. If you haven't touched that tennis racket since your "I could be the next Serena" phase in 2015, it's time to admit that you're more of a spectator than a player. Donate it to someone who will use it.

THE LINEN CLOSET

Linen closets are more like a magician's hat than a black hole—endlessly producing towels, sheets, and blankets you don't remember buying. If your sheets are so worn that they'd be more at home in a haunted house than on a bed, it's time to let them go. Thrift stores and local charities will happily take gently used linens, and any that are past their prime can go to animal shelters. Trust me, a rescue pup will appreciate that soft, threadbare sheet way more than you do. The same goes for towels and blankets that have seen better days. (Of course, animals deserve good linens too, if you'd rather go that route. I usually do. If it's soft or squishy, it goes to a good kitty or doggo in need.)

THE CLEANING CLOSET

Marketing gurus have you believing that every product solves one very specific problem and new products are inherently better than old ones. It's time to stop buying the hype—literally. Pick a multipurpose cleaner you like, use it on everything, and use it up. *Maybe* you want one with bleach and one without. But do you need a different one for every surface in your home? Absolutely not.

If you're someone who just likes to try new things, I'm going to need you to show a little restraint. Don't buy something new until you've used up whatever you already have. Does that new laundry detergent smell better than the old one? Sure. Does the old one smell bad? Of course not. You wouldn't have bought it in the first place if it did. So use it up, and then treat yourself to the one that smells like rain on a fall day.

There's a big difference between being prepared and hoarding.

Let's talk about hygiene products. Listen, we all lived through the pandemic. I'm not going to tell you not to stockpile toilet paper. (Though if you could leave some for the rest of us, that'd be super.) Just do it mindfully. Have extra, but don't let it take over your house or ruin your mental health. There's a big difference between being prepared and hoarding. Honestly, that's a mantra you can take with you throughout your decluttering adventures.

TAKE ACTION

This chapter is your first foray into the nitty-gritty of decluttering, and it's a lot. Don't let it overwhelm you. Just take it one step at a time.

- **START WITH TEN MINUTES.** You can't declutter an entire closet in ten minutes, but you can find a good yardstick item in that time. Start there.

- **SORT YOUR CLOTHES BY STYLE.** You can do this before or after you pile things up, but sorting your clothes helps you spot the repeats and extras more easily.

- **TRY THINGS ON.** If you're on the fence about something, try it on. If it's not an immediate "yes," then it's probably a "no."

UPGRADE YOUR KITCHEN AND BATH

HUMAN BEINGS ARE RESISTANT TO CHANGE, but boy, do we love an upgrade. The only difference between the two is in our mindset. When we *declutter* our stuff, we feel like we're losing a piece of ourselves. When we *upgrade* our stuff, we're embracing a new, better version of ourselves—and we're usually pretty happy to let go of the old version. And the two most frequently renovated rooms in a home are the kitchen and the bathroom—they get the highest return on investment. Why? Because they're the workhorses. That's a polite way of saying they're chock-full of stuff because we use them constantly. A new kitchen island or jetted tub might be lovely, but decluttering these spaces is the best upgrade you can give them. And it's free! Calmer, clearer, more useful spaces for just a bit of elbow grease? Talk about a return on investment.

THE KITCHEN OF YOUR DREAMS

The kitchen is a high-traffic zone, which means it's also a clutter magnet. You're cooking, eating, socializing, and even working in there. No wonder it's so full of stuff. But a clutter-free kitchen makes doing all of that so much easier. The first step? Pull it all out. Yes, all of it. Well, in batches of similar items anyway. You're going to want a large, clear space like a dining table or a covered section of the floor to spread everything out. Only when confronted by the truly ridiculous number of spatulas you've accumulated will you realize it's time to let some go.

EVERYDAY ITEMS

Be honest—how many mugs do you actually use? If you're someone who reaches for the same two or three favorites while the rest gather dust, it's time to thin the herd. The

> ### ⸂CLEAN AS YOU GO⸃
>
> If you're pulling everything out of your cabinets, fridge, and drawers, you may as well wipe things down as you go. (That includes the things you plan to donate—no thrift store employee should have to touch sticky cutlery.) You don't want to go through all this effort just to put your neatly edited collection of mugs back into a cabinet coated in crumbs from the early 2000s.

same goes for plates, bowls, and silverware. Your kitchen isn't a restaurant, so you don't need to stock enough dinnerware for a twenty-person party (especially if your kitchen table seats four and you prefer to eat takeout alone, in a sherpa-lined hoodie). Again, I say: declutter for the life you have, not the life you think you should have. Keep what you use regularly and maybe a few extras for guests, but let go of the chipped, mismatched, or just plain excessive pieces cluttering up your cabinets.

Not sure how many items to keep on hand? Ask yourself this: How many mugs, plates, glasses, and forks do you need to get to the next dishwasher cycle? If you constantly find yourself putting four mugs in the dishwasher before running it, that's probably how many you need. You can always run an extra cycle or—*gasp*—

light up when you hand them off? Obviously, you have to be ready to part with these gifts. We're not keeping things out of guilt, and we're not giving things away out of guilt either. But few feelings in life beat shared joy.

SHARE THE MEMORIES

The things you own are nothing without the memories and emotions you've attached to them. To anyone else looking at that necklace you keep tucked in your jewelry box, it's just a pretty piece of glass. To you, it's a reminder of how that vendor in Pompeii mistook your earnest "no thank you" for haggling and kept underbidding himself. (It was a steal at five dollars. How could you not bring it home?) If you get rid of that necklace, you can still share the memory of it. And you should.

As you go through your own things, invite your friends and family to learn more of your lore. Encourage them to ask questions. You'll often find that sharing the stories and emotions behind a piece helps you let go of it. And if you're helping someone else go through their things, be the one to ask questions. You never know what tawdry details you'll discover. Then the decluttering itself becomes a pretty great memory.

═TAKE ACTION

You'll probably feel the most resistance around things that fall into the sentimental category, so give yourself some grace. Start small, take breaks, make margaritas—whatever makes it easier.

- **SEE WHAT YOU'VE SET ASIDE.** If you've been following my sage advice, you've set aside a few sentimental things you weren't yet ready to declutter. Tackle those first.

- **GET CREATIVE.** Find one piece of sentimental clutter you've tucked away and give it new life where you can see and appreciate it. (If you're not feeling it after a while, you know you can let it go.)

- **START A CONVERSATION.** If you have an inheritor, call them up and ask them whether there's anything they'd really like to have. Their answer may surprise you.

9

TIE IT UP IN A BOW

THE FINAL PIECE OF THIS DEATH-CLEANING EXPERIENCE is to make sure you've tied up all the loose ends so your loved ones don't have to. That means dealing with everything you've decluttered, but it also means getting your affairs in order. Did everything in your body just contract like a vacuum-sealed bag? Whether you want to think about it or not, someone—your partner, your kids, your best friend, or some poor soul who barely knew you—will have to go through your things without you someday. The less junk you leave behind, the less they'll curse your name while sifting through boxes of expired warranties and mystery keys that unlock who-knows-what.

Death comes for us all. Even if it doesn't come for you for another forty years, you'll be glad you prepared for it now. And if you're not glad, take solace in the fact that your loved ones will be.

DEAL WITH THE EXCESS

This may surprise you, but you're not actually finished decluttering until the stuff is no longer in your home. "Sorted" and "decluttered" are not the same thing. Leaving eight unlabeled boxes in your guest room that you meant to take to the thrift store is no help to your loved ones, who will have to waste precious time and brain cells going through them. Deal with your stuff. Don't let something live rent-free in your home once you've decided it's not worth the space it's taking up.

ZONE BINS AND DOOM BOXES

Some organizing experts recommend keeping a small bin in each room to act as a catchall for anything that doesn't belong in that room. The idea is that you take the bin around your home at the end of the day or week, depositing things where they actually belong. Tossing things that don't belong into bins serves a dual purpose: it keeps everything together so you can put it all away at once, but it also clears your space so you don't get distracted or overwhelmed by visual clutter. (If you have ADHD, this can be a game changer.)

Don't let something live rent-free in your home once you've decided it's not worth the space it's taking up.

These boxes are not meant to be permanent depositories for all the random bits and bobs that don't seem to have a home or that you couldn't be bothered to put away. Those have their own delightful moniker: doom boxes. Imagine if the junk drawer multiplied and took up residence in every room in your house and you'll begin to understand doom boxes. Of course, if you're someone who defaults to using doom boxes, you don't have to imagine it. You're probably eyeballing one right now.

Put on some focus music or a true crime podcast— whatever gets you in a productive mood—and tackle a box. First, put away anything that actually has a home. Then deal with the leftovers. I've said it before, and I'll say it again: If it doesn't have a home, its home is probably in the trash. Mystery cords, old key cards, expired coupons, that one earring whose mate you haven't seen in years: trash.

HOME STORAGE

Just because you technically have the space to store the stuff does not mean you should keep the stuff. It's a cop-out—a way to avoid making decisions. One day, you look up, the clutter has taken over the space, and it's a much bigger problem. And what do we *not* do? Make it someone else's problem.

Think of all the places you've tucked things away to "deal with them later"—the garage, the attic, the basement, the crawl space, the closets, under beds, in those really high cupboards you never open because it

⸘RECLAIM THOSE SPACES⸛

What would you do with all that space in your basement if you weren't using it as clutter purgatory? I know a woman who loves movies so much that she turned her basement into a mini movie theater. It goes way beyond the standard home theater, too—I'm talking tiered leather recliners, top-of-the-line sound system, mini bar and pro-grade popcorn maker, and even those little strips of red lighting on the floor. Could she do that if she'd filled her basement with a lifetime's worth of emotional detritus? No. And she's much happier for it. Think about what you could do if you weren't holding on to yours.

would involve using a step stool. Now imagine someone going through your home after you're gone and, every time they think they've got a handle on the mess you've left them, finding another one of these little bastions of clutter. Even the most mellow person would be tempted to throw a lit match at the problem and walk away. (If that thought inspires in you some small amount of glee, just know that I am giving you my hardest stare.)

These spaces are magnets for the things that no longer fit into your life but that you hold on to because you haven't worked through all your emotional baggage. Good news: by now, you have! So, if you still haven't tackled those spaces, now is the time. Make those decisions now, little by little, and save everyone's sanity.

PAID STORAGE

Unless you live in an RV, a tiny home, or a tiny apartment (we're talking "New York City studio with a bed in the kitchen" tiny), you probably don't need a storage unit. Even the storage places know their rentals are a scam. That's why the 5 x 10 unit that cost you $80 per month when you moved your stuff in costs you $300 per month less than a year later. They lure you in with convenience, then jack up the price once you've filled the thing up. They know you'd rather chew off your own arm than declutter and downsize now that your home is blissfully free of all that stuff.

Here's what those shakedown artists won't tell you: if you're happy to have that stuff out of your home, then you probably don't need it. How often are you actually going to that storage unit to get things? Do you even know what's in there? Is it beach gear you're sure you need despite never taking more than a towel and a tote? Is it toys from your kids' childhood that they don't want but a children's charity might? Is it bins of photos you swear you'll put into an album someday?

Needing a storage unit from time to time is totally normal—life happens. Just don't let them suck you in. Stick it to the system by getting your stuff out of there as quickly as possible, then ditch the unit and put that money to better use. Treat yourself to an amazing vacation to celebrate your new lease on life. Maybe even hire a cleaning service to make your place sparkle once you've finished decluttering. But please, for the love of all things tidy, don't leave behind a storage unit full of junk for someone else to clean out after you're gone.

Death cleaning is just as much about taking responsibility for your stuff as it is about getting rid of it.

WHAT TO DO WITH IT ALL

Would it be easy to toss all your unwanted items in the trash and never think about them again? Sure. But you're not going to do that. You're going to take the time to make sure everything that can have a second life gets one. I know, you're exhausted. You just want to be done already. But we've talked about this—death cleaning is just as much about taking responsibility for your stuff as it is about getting rid of it.

It's not entirely selfless, though. You get the satisfaction of knowing that your unwanted stuff is making others happy and helping charitable organizations instead of contributing to overflowing landfills and floating garbage patches. That'll earn you bragging rights for at least a month. So, before you start hauling bags to the curb, let's talk about your options for gifting, donating, recycling, and selling your stuff like the responsible decluttering champ you are.

THINGS TO GIFT

You know better than to assume that your kids want your wedding dress or Grandma's hutch. But what about the good Dutch oven you don't use anymore or the sleeping bag you bought for that camping trip you never took? You probably have a ton of great, non-sentimental stuff that you want to make sure goes to a good home. That doesn't mean your friends and family will want it. All you can do is ask—politely. And be thoughtful in your offerings. Do not pressure, cajole, or cudgel people into taking your stuff or otherwise risk ruining your relationships over an air fryer. If the answer is no, there are plenty of places that are happy to take your clean, quality items.

THINGS TO DONATE

There's no shortage of places where you can donate those unwanted items that still have plenty of life left in them. The trick is figuring out where they'll do the most good. I've touched on a few of these solutions, but they bear repeating. Just keep in mind that these options aren't one-size-fits-all. Take a little time to find the best organizations in your city or town, and always call ahead before dropping things off. Donation centers fill up fast, and their needs change depending on the season, recent community drives, and how many other people are cleaning out their garages.

MEDIA

Libraries, schools, and thrift stores often welcome donations of books, DVDs, and CDs, which they'll sell to help raise funds. (These items don't go into circulation.) Most towns also have Little Free Libraries, which are adorable book-sharing boxes where you can pass along your books to new readers.

> ### ⸾DON'T DONATE TRASH⸾
>
> Donating items is a great way to assuage any lingering guilt during your death-cleaning escapades. You get to make some lucky thrifter happy instead of foisting unwanted stuff onto loved ones. But that's not an excuse to donate actual garbage to charitable organizations. That threadbare T-shirt? Those plastic fast-food cups? The office chair that's wonky because the lift is broken? Don't make donation centers throw those out for you. Your trash may be someone else's treasure, but it definitely shouldn't be someone else's problem. You can recycle some trash-adjacent items through the organizations I mention here. But if you can't, suck it up and throw them out. They had a good run.

FURNITURE

Organizations like Goodwill, the Salvation Army, and Habitat for Humanity's ReStore accept gently used furniture. If your piece is in great shape, you could also offer it up on a local "buy nothing" group or gift it to a local charity that helps furnish homes for families in need.

CLOTHING

Thrift stores, shelters, and community organizations will happily take clothing that's in good condition. (I repeat: in *good* condition.) Call ahead, though—some places have seasonal needs or specific donation policies.

LINENS AND PET ACCESSORIES

Animal shelters love old towels, sheets, and blankets. Even if they're a little threadbare for your bed, they're still a luxury for a rescue pup or kitten in need of a cozy place to sleep. And of course, they're happy to take any toys or accessories your pet has snubbed or outgrown.

> ### ⁝GOOD JARS AND TECH BOXES⁝
>
> You're allowed to repurpose your "good" jars, takeout containers, boxes, etc. with one caveat—you have to use them immediately. No saving them for a rainy day. There will always be another honey jar or phone box to fill the void.

(If you have cats, you know that decluttering their toys is a must—you buy endless amounts of mice and bells just for them to play with the packing paper.)

BROKEN BREAKABLES

That cracked vase or chipped dish set might not be donation-worthy, but rage rooms (places where people pay to smash things—seriously) could put them to good use. If there's one in your area, give them a call before you toss anything breakable.

THINGS TO RECYCLE

Just because it's not fit for donation doesn't mean it belongs in the trash. In fact, most items can be recycled. You just need to know where to take or send them. Here are some ideas for how to keep your discards out of the landfill. Again, a quick online search can help you find the best solutions in your area.

GLASS, PAPER, AND PLASTIC

Your local recycling center is the best place to start. Check your municipality's guidelines to see what they actually accept. (Because wishcycling—aka tossing stuff in the bin and *hoping* it gets recycled—is not the move.)

TECH, BATTERIES, INK, AND LIGHTBULBS

A lot of the bigger stores that sell electronics (Staples, IKEA, and Best Buy, for example) have designated drop-off spots for recycling these items responsibly. Some online programs will even send you a prepaid package to mail in your e-waste.

PHONES AND GLASSES

Plenty of organizations refurbish and redistribute these to people in need. Cellphone carriers and optometry offices often have collection bins, making it easy to drop off those outdated gadgets and glasses.

Perceived value and actual value are two very different things.

WORN-OUT CLOTHING

If your clothes are too far gone for donation, do a quick search for textile recycling programs. Some newer online companies let you send in items for a small fee, and they do the legwork of deciding how best to upcycle them. Or you could take a *very* local approach and use old clothes as cleaning rags instead of disposable mop pads or paper towels.

HARD-TO-RECYCLE ITEMS

Even with all of these options, some items are going to be tricky to recycle. Thankfully, organizations like TerraCycle are filling the gaps. TerraCycle specializes in collecting and repurposing things your municipality won't take, from snack wrappers to beauty product packaging, and they partner with a lot of well-loved brands to make it easy.

THINGS TO SELL

There's nothing wrong with trying to make a little money off your stuff—as long as you're willing to put in the work. That last part's important. Selling stuff is harder than it looks. Just ask anyone who's ever worked retail and had a customer get in their face over a clearly marked price. And here's the kicker: none of your stuff is worth as much money as you think it is. (OK, some things are. But I doubt you've got a mint-condition *Amazing Spider-Man* issue #300 comic book hiding in your sock drawer.)

Perceived value and actual value are two very different things. Most of the things we thought would appreciate over the years—dishware from the 1930s, hand-carved wooden furniture, that Princess Diana Beanie Baby—sit untouched in antique stores for lack of demand. (Yes, even the Beanie Baby.) Convenience and cost often win over quality. Why haul a heavy, solid-wood dresser upstairs when you can tote a few boxes up and build one that's lighter and has soft-close drawers?

You also have to contend with bargain hunters. People expect a deal when it comes to secondhand stuff. Selling yours online has never been easier, but that's kind of the problem. Your vintage American Flyer Hudson train is one of a dozen on the market for a range of prices. Unless you can beat all of them or offer something unique, you're probably out of luck. And yard sales are a lot of work for not a lot of payoff (unless you enjoy standing in the hot sun all day with strangers and selling your fishing rods for 50 cents apiece).

⋛ SELL SMART ⋚

Before you put time and effort into listing your stuff for sale, do a little research. Find out whether there's a market for it and how much people have paid for similar items. A quick internet search is a good start. If you're selling on a website or app built for the purpose, you can usually sort listings by "sold" to see how much others have gotten for the same item. And if you can't be bothered to do any of that, just drive your stuff over to the thrift store now. Sales is not for you.

So, what can you sell? Anything you want to. Just go into it with your eyes open, knowing that you'll probably end up frustrated and wanting to leave most stuff on the curb. If you've got nothing but time and wouldn't mind an extra ten dollars here and there, give it a go. If you've got something of actual, quantifiable value on your hands and want to make the rounds to every reseller in the area, great. But if you're already slammed and just want your stuff gone, donation can't be beat. Being able to drop off your unwanted (*yet clean and working*) toaster, knowing someone else is going to love discovering it among aisles of jam jars, and helping out a good cause? That's priceless.

THINGS TO TRADE

Remember when neighbors would just loan each other what they needed instead of ordering it with two-day shipping? (If this concept is completely foreign to you, go watch a few episodes of any 1960s sitcom and come back.) It doesn't happen much anymore, but local "no sell" and "buy nothing" groups are trying to bring it back. These are online forums where you can post that you have an extra leaf blower you don't need, and someone else who does need it will take it off your hands. You might trade it for their unwanted (yet clean and working) toaster, or you might get nothing in return. The point is to help your fellow human and buck the trend of rampant consumerism that got us all into this mess in the first place. Find groups near you with a quick internet or social-media search.

You've already made the tough decisions. Trust yourself, and drop off that box ASAP.

GET RID OF STUFF QUICKLY

Whatever your plans for it are, don't let that box of stuff sit around long enough for you to forget what's in it. When your curiosity inevitably gets the better of you, you'll go through the box and start pulling stuff out. That little rush of rediscovering "lost" things will make you want to keep them. Don't fall into the trap. Three years later, when your clutter grows to untenable levels again, you'll be packing those things into yet another donation box. You've already made the tough decisions. You put those wired headphones in there for good reason (aka none of your devices have headphone jacks anymore). Trust yourself, and drop off that box ASAP.

GET YOUR DUCKS IN A ROW

Congratulations! You've *actually* finished decluttering. Sit back and admire your work—you've earned some downtime. Enjoy your well-deserved sense of accomplishment (and maybe a cold beverage in the sunroom you can now use because it's not full of junk). When you're ready, come back and we'll finish this thing. Oh, you thought you were done? Did you not notice there are several pages left in this book?

⸢HIRE A LAWYER⸥

I have no problem advising you on tossing your junk mail, cleaning out your desk drawers, and organizing your papers into some recognizable semblance of order. But I can't help you draw up a will, prepare your legal estate, establish your final wishes, set up trusts, or help your inheritors avoid a long, drawn-out probate (which will keep them from settling your estate). For that, you need a good lawyer. You should hire one—sooner rather than later. Do I hear you arguing about having plenty of time? I thought we were past that. Once you set everything up, you can update it as things change. But if you wait until it's too late, your kids will be stuck paying their mortgage *and* yours while the wheels of justice slowly churn.

OK, now that you're back, let's talk about the *final* step: getting your affairs in order so no one has to play detective with your stuff when you're gone. You've done most of the legwork by whittling things down. Now you just have to think ahead to what happens to it after you're gone.

This is your life. (And your death.)
Take responsibility for it.

TAKE CARE OF BUSINESS

It may be morbid, but death is a business. From medical care to estate planning to funeral services and more, there are a lot of costly decisions and preparations to be made. And *you* have to make them. Don't leave this stuff up to your loved ones. They're grieving you (presumably). And every decision they have to make will feel like a test of how much they knew and loved you—a test they're failing because they're so overwhelmed by the weight of it all that they couldn't even tell you their own eye color anymore.

This is your life. (And your death.) Take responsibility for it. Start by making sure important documents—wills, insurance info, passwords—are easy to find. (This should be easy because you've already gone through everything.

Right? *Right*?) For karmic bonus points, make your final arrangements in advance. At minimum, have the hard conversations with the people in your life about what you want in death so they don't have to guess.

PLAN FOR YOUR REMAINING STUFF

You've tackled the clutter, so everything that's left is integral to either your happiness or your existence. (You're nodding, yes?) But not all things are created equal. Don't leave your loved ones guessing about whether that cat-in-glasses print was a treasured piece or a cute thrift-store find. Just tell them flat out. Knowing where things land in your hierarchy of happiness can ease the burden they feel in trying to honor your life.

⋛WARN A PERSON⋚

If there's anything you want to keep but wouldn't want your loved ones to find (you know what I'm talking about), put it in a box and label it with a warning. Something like, "Do Not Open" should suffice. Adding a lock would be better. If you know your offspring are nosy, you could label it something they'd be likely to throw out, like "appliance manuals" or "spare buttons." Of course, you run the risk of their curiosity getting the better of them. But that's on them. You're dead. What do you care?

Let inheritors know what's worth keeping, what meant a lot to you, and what can go straight to the donation bin. You could do this by dropping the info into casual conversation, but neither one of you is likely to remember it later. The better option is to put it in writing, either in a document (physical or digital) or by labeling the things themselves. (I've never met a better use of a label maker.) Take it a step further and let them know about the great places you've found to donate the stuff that can go when you do. And make sure you call out any valuables lest some lucky thrifter find your super-rare commemorative Elvis plates on sale for 50 cents next to someone's used yoga mat. Anything that's actually worth money should be listed in your will or put into a trust, though. (Again, you'll need a lawyer for that. I'm just here to tell you to throw out your ratty underwear before your kids see it.)

This is exactly why we declutter ahead of time—so this part is quick and painless. If something is truly meaningful, make it obvious. If you realize while making these arrangements that some things are still taking up space out of guilt or laziness, let them go now. Make it a habit. Update your space and your documents every six months, or once a year on the anniversary of your divorce. Whatever motivates you. Because the best gift you can give your loved ones isn't a thing; it's the peace of knowing exactly what to do when the time comes.

TAKE ACTION

You've accomplished so much—keep up that momentum! You'll feel amazing once all that extra stuff is gone.

- **FIND SOME FAVORITE TAKERS.** Do a search in your area for donation and recycling options. Who knows, you might have something fun, like an upcycling center that takes the scraps left over from your crafting and DIY escapades.

- **TALK TO YOUR LOVED ONES.** It's tough to have conversations about death, but it beats wishing you had. You don't need to hash everything out at once. Just start.

- **REST.** Decluttering is exhausting. Make sure you're taking the time you need to rest between sprints and when you're finished for the day.

KEEP MOVING FORWARD

LOOK AT YOU. Look how far you've come! It takes courage to admit you're not where you want to be in life and to make a change. You've not only finished this book, but you've also (hopefully) opened yourself up to some new perspectives. Maybe you've started decluttering along the way. Or maybe you've been putting every section into practice and you're enjoying a clutter-free life right now. No matter where you are in your journey, you've put in the effort, challenged old habits, made new ones, and shown yourself what you're capable of. Keep moving forward, keep learning, and most importantly, keep making room for what truly matters. Just keep in mind the lessons you've learned along the way so you don't repeat clutter history. (You've done the hard work—at this point, you only have yourself to blame if you have to do it all again.)

WE ALL HAVE TOO MUCH STUFF

No one is immune to clutter. It sneaks in through impulse purchases, sentimental attachments, and sheer laziness. But now you know better. You've seen firsthand that stuff doesn't add meaning to your life. It can, however, add stress. So, keep the purchases to a minimum and just say no when someone offers you a freebie you don't need.

CLUTTER IS EMOTIONAL

Decluttering isn't just about getting rid of things—it's also about confronting the *reasons* behind them. Are you holding on to something out of guilt? Obligation? Fear of change? The emotional weight of clutter can be just as heavy as the physical mess, but now you're better equipped to lighten that load. When you feel yourself resisting, get to the bottom of it.

GUILT IS WORTHLESS

Whether it's gifts you didn't like, expensive mistakes, or family heirlooms you don't actually want, keeping things out of guilt is just a way of punishing yourself. You deserve better than that. Keep the empathy, but toss the guilt and anything that evokes it.

HAPPY IS BETTER THAN PERFECT

Forget the Pinterest-worthy, hyper-organized homes that look like no one actually lives in them. You're creating a space that *works* for you—a space where you can breathe, relax, and enjoy life without feeling like you're drowning in a sea of perfectly labeled storage bins. Let happiness be your guide. (Unless it's guiding you toward shopping for a quick dopamine hit. Then let common sense be your guide.)

MEMORIES MATTER, THINGS DON'T

You don't need a cluttered home to prove you've had a full life. The people, experiences, and relationships that shaped you aren't tied to the physical objects you've been holding on to. Practice gratitude for how those sentimental items served their purpose, then let them go.

COMMUNICATION IS KEY

Clutter doesn't just affect you—it also impacts the people you live with, the ones you'll eventually leave things to, and the ones who'll have to clean up what's left. Having honest conversations about what stays, what goes, and who actually wants what can spare everyone a lot of stress.

YOU'RE RESPONSIBLE FOR YOUR STUFF

You got yourself into this mess, and you're getting yourself out of it. You're making the tough decluttering decisions. You're donating, recycling, and upcycling responsibly. Now you just have to start making more mindful choices about what you bring in so you don't have to keep fighting the same battles.

Every day that you wake up is a fresh start, a new opportunity to carve out a little more happiness.

YOU'RE NEVER ACTUALLY FINISHED

Decluttering isn't a one-and-done deal. Stuff will keep creeping in, life will keep changing, and you'll need to adjust. But don't let that fact give you heartburn. It's not a bad thing. Just like learning, growing, and finding joy, decluttering is a lifelong process. Tomorrow isn't guaranteed. But every day that you wake up is a fresh start, a new opportunity to carve out a little more happiness. Embrace it!

YOU CAN'T TAKE IT WITH YOU

Death cleaning was never about the stuff—it's about releasing control over what happens to it after you're gone. You can't micromanage your legacy from beyond the grave. At the end of the day, and at the end of our lives, what really matters are the people we've loved and who have loved us. We want the best for them. And that means breaking the cycle of stuff once and for all. Let go. Then let them let go, too.

⟹ *TAKE ACTION*

Even if you've done the bulk of the decluttering, there are a few easy things you can do to maintain your sparser space. And if you've yet to start, these tips will also help you along the way.

- **STOP BUYING STUFF.** Remember, it's the memories that count. Consider how you might put your money toward making new memories instead of buying new stuff.

- **COME BACK TO WHY.** When you're exhausted or just over this whole decluttering thing, remember why you're doing it. Think of what got you moving in the first place, or pick a new motivator from the list.

- **KEEP UP THE GOOD WORK.** If you've worked through this book, you've pretty much trained your brain to default to decluttering. That means you'll start seeing decluttering moments everywhere. You'll notice things you don't love anymore, things you think other people will love more, and things you don't need to buy. Lean in.

- **BONUS:** Help others see the (unobstructed) light. If you're decluttering because you're terrified of inheriting someone else's mess, now is the time to talk to them about decluttering. Or you can just hand them this book—I'm happy to do the talking for you.

INDEX

acceptance, 16–17
accessories, 85
accounts, 123–124
alarms, 127
anger, 14–15
antiques, 140
anxiety, 67
aphantasia, 46
apps, 125
aspirational clutter, 69–70

baby clothes, 141
bags, 83–85
bargaining, 15
basements, 150
bathrooms, 94–95, 104–110
batteries, 158
bedroom closets, 72–88
bedrooms, 73, 88–89
belts, 85
best-by dates, 100
billing statements, 115
bins, 148–149
blankets, 91
body doubling, 58
books, 98–99, 134, 155
boundary setting, 143–144
boxes, 42, 156
brain dumps, 47–48
browser tabs, 127, 128
buyer's remorse, 60
"buy nothing" groups, 161–162

capsule wardrobe, 76–77
change, 21–23
cleaning
    closets, 92–93
    kitchens, 96
    time spent, 29–30
closets, 89–90
    bedroom, 72–88
    cleaning, 92–93
    emptying, 74–75

hall, 90–91
    linen, 91
clothes, 73–82, 156, 158
clutter magnets, hidden, 67–68
coats, 90
commitment, 70–71
computer files, 11–12, 118–123, 128
cookbooks, 98–99
cords, 115–116
cosmetics, 108–109
costs, of keeping stuff, 50–51
cultural values, 140
cupboard shelves, 103–104
cutting boards, 98

death cleaning
    overview of, 6–8
    stages of, 12–17
decision fatigue, 57
decision making
    enlisting help for, 51–52
    five-second approach to, 49–50
    system for, 37–42
decision paralysis, 16
denial, 13–14
despair, 15–16
digital files, 111–112, 118–123, 128
digital password managers, 122
dishware, 95–96, 103
distractions, 54, 128
documents, 114–115, 128, 164–165
    See also digital files
donating items, 153–157, 161, 166, 167
doom boxes, 148–149
downloads, 127–128
80/20 rule, 77–78, 83
electronics recycling, 158
emails, 119, 120–121
emotions, 18, 145, 169
energy, 89
estate planning, 163, 164–165
everyday items, 95–97
expiration dates, 100
extraneous items, 34

174   YOU CAN'T TAKE IT WITH YOU

family fights, 140–142
fast fashion, 73, 80
feng shui, 89
final arrangements, 164–167
first pass, 35–42
five-minute approach, 53–54
five-second approach, 49–50
food, 99–100
friends, decluttering with, 51–52, 58
furniture donations, 156

gifting items, 154
glasses, 158
glass recycling, 157
goals
  making progress toward, 61
  realistic, 59–61
gratitude, 69, 170
guilt, 14, 24, 70, 133, 138, 139, 145, 166, 169–170
gut reactions, 37–42, 50

habit formation, 57–58
hall closets, 90–91
happiness, 34, 38–39, 68, 170
heirlooms, 140–143, 169
hidden stuff, 66–67
holiday decor, 132
home office, 112–118
home storage, 150–151
hygiene products, 92–93

inbox zero, 120
inventory, taking, 35–37, 42

jackets, 90
jars, 156
jewelry, 85–87
junk drawers, 102
junk mail, 113–114

kitchen gadgets, 97
kitchens, 94–104, 110

lawyers, 163, 166
legacy contact, 124

libraries, 155
linen closets, 91
linens, 90, 91, 109, 156
loose ends, 147–167
loved ones
  asking, about sentimental items, 140–144
  communicating with, 80, 138–143, 154, 170–171
  decluttering to benefit, 23–25, 138–139
luggage, 84

media, 155
medicine cabinets, 105–106
me-focused motivators, 20–23
memories, 130, 131, 132, 135, 145, 170, 173
mental health, 17–18, 67, 69, 93
mental load, 27–29
messages, 126
mess-focused motivators, 26–31
mini toiletries, 108
mortality, 31–32
motivation, 19–32, 70
  me-focused, 20–23
  mess-focused, 26–31
  them-focused, 23–25
moving, 30–31, 55–56, 133
mugs, 95

napkins, 101
nightstands, 88–89
"no sell" groups, 161–162
nostalgia, 131–132
notifications, 128

office space, 112–118, 128
office supplies, 117–118, 128
online resellers, 86, 160
organizational systems, 67–68
overthinkers, tips for, 49–53

paid storage, 151–152
pantries, 99–100
paper recycling, 157

papers, 113–115
paper shredders, 114
passwords, 121–123, 164
perfectionism, 53
perfectionists, tips for, 59–61
personal style, 75–76
pet accessories, 156–157
phones, 54, 124–128, 158
photos, 119, 126, 132
pictures, before and after, 62
planning, 47–48
plastic recycling, 157
prescriptions, 106
printers, 116
priorities, changing, 63–64
probate, 163
procrastinators, tips for, 53–56
purses, 83–85

rage rooms, 157
rating system, 50
realistic goals, 59–61
recycling, 80, 116, 157–159, 167
refrigerators, 99–100
reminders, 127
reusable shopping bags, 101

sauces, 101
scarcity mindset, 28
seasonal decluttering, 65–66, 79
seasonal decor, 132
self-care, decluttering as, 20–21
sell-by dates, 100
selling items, 159–161
sentimental items, 64, 72, 129–146, 170
sheets, 90, 91
shoes, 83
shopping, 78, 173
shredders, 114
silverware, 96
slippers, 85
small tasks, 54–55
smartphones, 54, 124–128, 158
socks, 79–80

space
  hushing the, 68
  loving your, 20–21
  planning your, 47–48
  reimagining your, 44–46
  storage, 23, 136–137, 150–152
sports gear, 91
storage bins, 88
storage space, 23, 136–137, 150–152
storage units, 151–152
structure lovers, tips for, 56–58

takeout menus, 101
technology
  changing, 22
  getting rid of outdated, 115–117
  recycling, 158
textile recycling, 80, 158
text threads, 126
them-focused motivators, 23–25
tidying up, 39
time blocking, 57
toiletries, 107–108
towels, 91, 109
trades, 161–162

umbrellas, 90–91
under-bed storage, 89
upgrades, 94–95
utensils, 101

visual inventory, 36–37
visualization
  aids, 46
  of dream home, 45
visual learners, tips for, 61–63
visual noise, 68, 149

wardrobe, 73–82
water bottles, 101
wedding dresses, 141
wills, 163, 164, 166

yard sales, 160
yardsticks, 62–63, 74, 93

zone bins, 148–149